IS ANYBODY THERE?

IS ANYBODY THERE?

STEWART LAMONT

MAINSTREAM
PUBLISHING
—Edinburgh—

First published in Great Britain by
MAINSTREAM PUBLISHING COMPANY (EDINBURGH) LTD.,
28 Barony Street, Edinburgh EH3 6NY.

ISBN 0 906391 11 3

Contents

Foreword

Substance of the Matter

When we were considering titles for a BBC television series on the paranormal, I suggested that "Out of Their Minds?" might be appropriate. First because people might think that those who produce or witness psychic phenomena do so as a result of some temporary or chronic distortion of their perception. Second, I had come to believe that most of the range of psychic phenomena (ghosts, seances, metal-bending, poltergeists) can be linked to the state of mind of the agents who produce them or the people who witness them. But the discussion about titles took place after we had filmed the series and long after I had first reflected on this twilight world of mind and matter. So in a sense by asking the question about the link between mind and matter, I was assuming acceptance of psychic phenomena at a time when many people still need to be convinced that they exist.

In the end a much more fundamental and appropriate question became the title — "Is Anybody There?" (or in the case of some of the programmes — "Is Anything There?"). In the series we were trying to set out the evidence for six areas of psychic phenomena, reflect on them a little, and leave the viewer to decide. The six areas were Poltergeists, Ghosts, Survival (of Death), Reincarnation, Clairvoyance, and Psychokinesis (mind-over-matter effects such as healing and metal-bending).

Despite the strange nature of many of these subjects, the number of people who have some experience of them is considerable. It is said that one in eight of the population has seen a ghost and an equally large proportion have attended a seance of some sort during their lives. Even the ultra-sceptical

5

attitude of the *New Scientist* was fractured in 1969 by a poll among its readers in which only three per cent declared that psychic phenomena definitely did not exist.

Trial by television is not usually meant as a compliment. It suggests that the case is "loaded" in a rhetorical way. Besides, psychic phenomena are rarely captured on permanent record: most of the testimony is verbal, and television prefers visual evidence. In making "Is Anybody There?" we were lucky on two counts, in two important areas.

In the case of most of the phenomena, such as the "past lives" recalled under hypnosis, there are a number of possible explanations. But both poltergeists and metal-bending involve measurable *physical* effects, which cannot be explained away as subjective delusion. Either a poltergeist caused a flowerpot to shoot across a room — or someone threw it. Either it was psychokinetic force that bent a spoon as a teenage boy stroked it — or he gave it a twist when no one was looking. There are only two alternatives: one is trickery, the other is a genuine paranormal event.

The first programme considered the case for poltergeists. As well as verbal testimonies there were three powerful pieces of evidence. The bulk of the film was shot at Enfield in Essex in February 1978, when a poltergeist was active in the home of the Hodgson family. The principal investigators claim that this case is one of the "classics of all time". Although newspaper and radio journalists visited the home, ours remains the only film record of the poltergeist while it was active.

It included film of two girls speaking in the gruff "devil" voices which the investigators claim could not be ventriloquised for the long periods managed by the girls; knocking on the wall (typical of poltergeist cases) which occurred during my interviews with the girls who appeared to be the focus of the poltergeist activity (all the family were under observation at the time); and a series of stills taken by Graham Morris, a freelance photographer, which show the girls levitating in their bedroom: the camera was triggered remotely and took several pictures at 1/6 second intervals, showing the girls rising into the air.

These rare photographs will undoubtedly be the subject of controversy (as are the "voices") but the range of poltergeist phenomena witnessed at Enfield add up to an impressive file of evidence. However, this does not provide a simple "Yes" answer to the question "Is Anybody There?". The behaviour of a poltergeist — intelligent vandalism, throwing objects around a house, sometimes ingeniously hiding them — often resembles the pranks of the adolescents who are the "focus" of the activity. Even if we eliminate tricks as an explanation, the notion of a separate entity must be questioned. It is more likely that the poltergeist is a product of the child mind(s), a force which draws its personality from them.

The subject of metal-bending is inextricably linked with Uri Geller, who is tied up with show business and performs his feats professionally. Both these factors make him a doubtful subject for the investigator of the paranormal, because they raise too many questions about his motives. It would be much better if someone without these incentives could replicate his feats. Sixteen-year-old Stephen North of London did just that for our cameras. He produced signals on strain gauges in the laboratory, just by holding his hands near to them without touching. The effect had been video-filmed by Professor John Hasted at Birkbeck College, but when outside media men turn up, the "shyness effect" tends to come into operation—the bending only occurs when the camera is not running. Fortunately Garry Morrison, our gifted cameraman, managed to establish a rapport with Stephen. This produced rare shots of him stroking a fork, which behaved like plasticine in his hands. Although this effect has the same "delinquent" features as the poltergeist event, we do not suggest that there are "demons" bending the cutlery. Thus the appropriate question in both cases may be "Is Anything There?".

The area of psychic research which has most implications for our destiny, purpose and religious faith is Survival of Death. Improved resuscitation techniques in hospitals have increased the number of "near-death" patients who came back to tell the tale. They have a remarkable correspondence in their tales (experiences of a "being of light", going into a "tunnel" and looking down on their own body). This is thought to be a *prima facie* case for something existing independently of the body, which might be able to travel out of the body.

The next step is to look at the areas of evidence of survival. There are the composers (like Rosemary Brown) and artists (Luis Gasparetto) who compose in the style of the dead masters yet in themselves do not apparently have the ability to produce such work. There are the mediums who can produce letters in languages unknown to them and messages from people not known to be dead. Yet they sometimes make mistakes or completely miss the mark. Why? Is the human factor imperfectly transmitting the information given to them by the dead — or is it just that the information was "dreamed up" by the medium in the first place with the help of telepathic droplets of information, rather than spirits?

In the case of reincarnation, the memory bank of an adult could also be said to "dream up" the personality of a past life into a daytime fantasy. For the television series I underwent a session of hypnotic "regression" and produced two "past lives", one as a Viking chieftain and the other as an uncouth Scots farm labourer. The latter was able to speak in dialect which I can mimic in my waking moments, so why not when in trance? Why not indeed? for although I found the experience quite entertaining, I was not convinced that I was communicating a past life. My two alter egos did not supply any startling information about themselves and were rather too like aspects of my own personality — or so I was told by my friends. This even further confused me about the question of collective unconscious, the theoretical ocean into which each individual stream of thought flows.

I needed to reflect on the possible explanations and match them to the phenomena which I had seen and the well-authenticated cases I had read about. In many ways I found the medium of television inadequate for this. Television documentaries illuminate areas of a subject and they entertain. By their nature they have to exclude certain aspects which would require pictures to illustrate or accompany the spoken content. The visual nature of the medium also means that what cannot be shown will have less prominence than something which has a photogenic side to it. (Thus we left out Astrology, which was too dependent on technical explanations.) Another factor is the number of people involved in making the series — a series producer, a producer, two directors, a film cameraman and crew of three, a film editor — all adding, subtracting or modifying the material which the scriptwriter or presenter wants to get across to the audience. This can result in an absurd situation where you have twelve seconds to explain the problem of survival evidence, accompanied by a shot of a medium sitting at a table. The medium herself may then furnish a shot. But in the final assembly the "talking head" will be omitted to make room for film of a psychic artist in full flight, even though an assessment of his ambiguous evidence is less easy. He is more entertaining.

I do not wish to criticise any of the people involved. They are right to insist that their programmes are polished and entertaining — that is why the rest of us watch them. That is why they are given the large sums of money needed to make television programmes. We, the audience, on the whole get the television we ask for.

But there are other, technical limitations in the use of television. Reels of film only hold ten minutes; it is impossible to film beneath a certain level of lighting without special equipment; the camera cannot suddenly spin round to cover something which happens in a corner of the room not covered by the brilliant lights. Psychic phenomena do not have the slightest respect for these limitations.

Coming to television after eight years as a BBC radio producer, I was only too aware of these limitations, for on radio you can speak about the most important things first (not necessarily those which have the most exciting pictures to "hold" the viewer). The unobtrusive radio microphone can eavesdrop on events without influencing them, and the English language has a range which can adequately describe the phenomena. Having said that, I have to admit that television still wins hands down when it comes to portraying the intriguing wonders of the paranormal world. It is surprising that there are not more television programmes on the subject. Perhaps the electronic tricks displayed to such dazzling effect on "Top of the Pops" would be too easy to employ. Or is it that the lobby against anything which smacks of the "Occult" influences the TV moguls to regard psychic phenomena as a pornography of the mind?

I doubt whether either of these explanations is correct, but the shortage of television material is an interesting contrast to the explosion in paperbacks about the paranormal during the nineteen-seventies. Apart from the excellent "Leap in the Dark" series, which dramatised historic cases, there has been precious little in the way of documentary work to reflect the upsurge in public interest and in research findings. Occasionally "Nationwide" would venture into the field, but it was ironic that in 1978 it was easier to get money to make a drama series

9

("The Omega Factor"), which gave a weird and far-fetched picture of parapsychology, than to get money for documentaries which would explore some of the fascinating results being produced by mediums, metal-benders and telepaths immersed in the "Ganzfeld". When money was forth-coming, there was a great deal which could have been included which has not been covered before.

Another limitation of both radio and television is that they are ephemeral. The video-cassette recorder (VCR) is rapidly changing this, but it is sad that once seen, even if not forgotten, a programme cannot be summoned back to scrutinise its content unless it is repeated. Whereas it is more appropriate for the psychic detective to be able to re-scrutinise his clues before coming to any conclusion rather than have them paraded before his eyes and ears at sixteen frames per second of film or fifteen inches per second of recording tape. A page can be summoned back rather more easily. That is what drove me into print — partly to cover more ground than the series had done, and in greater detail, and partly to work out in greater depth the questions (and answers) which had suggested themselves to me.

It would be a bold man or a foolish one who ventured definitive answers to psychic phenomena. The best that I can offer is a paradigm, and a rather old theory. The theory is that we are prevented from being able to assess the true essence or "form" of the world by the limitations of sequential time and the physical senses connected to the brain. Mind exists independent of both the physical senses and the tick-tock of our bodily clock, the pulse which tells us we are alive. That idea is hardly new and found favour among the Greeks. At least I can claim that the paradigm is relatively modern.

Imagine that the brain is like a coiled roll of film. Naively we might imagine that our memories are printed onto it photo-graphically, and can be replayed when we need them. But what happens when we replay the picture of a loved one? We see them as something different than flesh and blood. The picture has been coloured by *value*, meaningful and moral. Thus it is not a mechanical process but one which is influenced by factors that are outside bodily functions of space and time. The paranormal is not an interruption of these functions, or of Natural Law. It is not a miracle. I have just finished listening to a Mozart violin concerto. I end up awestruck, not by the technical brilliance of the player, although I admire it, but by the essence of music. When I look back over the rolls of film about the paranormal on the VCR, I am intrigued by the mechanics which go into making a film, fascinated by the peculiarities of the phenomena, but ultimately I am given a glimpse of something which TV eye hath not seen nor clair-audient ear heard. In other words, I do not see the paranormal as a crutch to prop up my religious belief, but one of the senses by which it is experienced.

Chapter One

Do You Mind?—Poltergeists

Poltergeist. The word is German and means, literally, "noise spirit". But what kind of spirit? According to the psychic researchers Andrew Lang and Frank Podmore, around the turn of the century, the presence of a poltergeist was indicated either by unexplained noises (raps, bangs, or sawing noises), by the movement of objects by no known physical means, or by a combination of both. But as we shall see when we consider four recent cases, the poltergeist often exhibits many more spectacular features which shed new light on this strange phenomenon, even if they do not explain it.

Poltergeists are not an invention of the Society for Psychical Research to keep its members occupied. Luther alludes to them; so does Milton, at a point in *L'Allegro* when much ale is consumed:

> With stories told of many a feat
> How fairy Mab the junkets eat;
> She was pinched—pulled she said.

This mischievous pinching and pulling (identified in this myth with fairies) is a common feature of poltergeist activity. Other features, found in cases from all over the world, have included fire-raising of a spontaneous nature; hurling of objects in abnormal trajectories (called Lithobolia); writing on walls and marks like scratches appearing on flesh; levitation and traction of persons as well as objects; apports (the apparent dematerialisation of objects which reappear in another place, sometimes in a locked room and often warm to the touch); the sound of voices, in some cases speaking through persons; apparitions of people (some of them still living) and of strange

12

lights; and the spontaneous appearance of liquids on floors and through ceilings, and vile smells.

Readers of accounts of witchcraft trials in the Middle Ages will recognise many of the symptoms which I have listed as appearing in garbled form in the rolls of charges against witches. For although poltergeists affect places which are then thought to be "haunted", they are invariably linked to a person or persons and (if trickery is eliminated) the tendency is to conclude that the person is producing the phenomena by occult means. Trials of witches were more common than trials of their male counterparts, and it is not surprising to find that three of the four classic cases of recent years involve girls, who appear to be more susceptible to psychic phenomena (the ratio is about two to one).

Current cases of psychic phenomena are even more fascinating than those of yesteryear, because witnesses are still available for cross-checking, because phenomena are still active or have been recorded on tape or film, or simply because there are more grounds for accepting the existence of incredible happenings if they are current and not just buried in the past.

One of the most spectacular supernatural stories of recent years has been *The Amityville Horror*, which is the subject and title of a book by Jay Anson. In December 1975, George and Kathy Lutz, a young couple with a family of three, bought a dream home in Amityville, Long Island. The house had been the scene of a multiple murder in November 1974, when Ronald Defeo had slaughtered his family of six. Within a month of moving in the Lutz family had fled, abandoning their possessions and refusing to return. Locked windows and doors were blown open, there were plagues of flies, vile smells of excrement, and ghostly visitations — one apparently of Defeo himself, witnessed by a priest who had come to perform an exorcism. The Lutz family were afraid to speak about their experiences for two years, and their reluctance perhaps enhances the credibility of their story. But no proper investigation or evaluation of the phenomena was made at the time and it does not qualify as a classic case. Even though many of the hallmarks of the poltergeist are present in the story, without more corroboration it is too easy for the sceptic to dismiss it on the grounds that the previous history of the house may have influenced the Lutzs' imagination. Questionable though that the Amityville episode may be then, there are nevertheless many more substantiated poltergeist incidents, as the following four cases exemplify.

The first happened in 1960 in the village of Sauchie in Clackmannanshire, Scotland. A fourteen-year-old girl, Virginia Campbell, had moved from her home on a croft in County Donegal, Ireland, to a council house at 19 Park Crescent, Sauchie, where her older brother lived with his wife and daughter Margaret. Virginia's father was selling his croft and was to follow, while her mother was "living in" at her place of employment a few miles away in Dollar. Knocks and bumps first started in November when the two girls went to bed. On 14 December, Virginia's sister-in-law wrote in her diary:

> Virginia was in the house with dad. He said while I was away an apple came out of the dish three times. The clock came off the cabinet and hit Virginia on the nose, settled on the chair just before I came back. A piece of chocolate jumped off the sideboard, also a pencil. A brillo pad came out of the kitchen into the living room. The light went on twice. Virginia was using the (vacuum) cleaner. It went off and the rubber flew off the handle. A doll came off the chest of drawers on to the bed a few times. A flower came out of the vase at the bottom of the stairs. A chair tumbled over. There was a little knocking on the big chair. A table drawer opened. The cupboard door opened and the table kept moving. Then there was a knocking on the table. Virginia gave three knocks and there was three knocks back. . . . At dinner the table moved again, knocking on the cupboard door. Virginia was getting pinched on the side. . . . The top of Margaret's hot water bag was opened and there was a little scraping. The girls got nipped in bed. . . . Virginia's leg was getting tickled. . . . For the past three nights there has been writing on the girl's face. The bedcover turned red. It was a green cover. There was a noise like somebody walking across the floor. Virginia's lips went bright red three times and there was a noise like a ball bouncing.

Several of the classic features of the poltergeist are already present in this account. The local minister, the Rev. T. W. Lund, and the two family doctors, Dr Nisbet and Dr Logan, were called in. They witnessed the rappings and sawing noises,

14

which Dr Logan recorded on his tape recorder. As Virginia lay in bed, under observation, a linen chest flew open. The bed-clothes started rippling like a pond in a stiff wind while Virginia's hands were visible on top. Dr Logan himself tried to make a similar movement when he got home but found it impossible. The pillow beside Virginia's bed turned through ninety degrees while under observation. Some of the phenomena followed Virginia to school and were witnessed by Miss Margaret Stewart, her teacher. Doors flew open, a desk rose in the air and Miss Stewart's pointer began to vibrate on the desk beside her. All these incidents occurred at separate times over a period of a few months. Mostly they were witnessed by one or more people; sometimes Virginia was under observation at the time. She was examined medically and found to be in normal physical and mental condition for a girl of her age.

That last phrase is significant in that poltergeist activity very often centres on adolescents. They are sometimes called the "focus" and the phenomena are liable to take place only when they are in the vicinity (although this is not always the case, as we shall see later). It is possible that some process in the body which coincides with pubescence triggers off some force, a kind of "mental whirlwind" which comes from the child who is the "focus", but this does not explain why pubescent girls are not more frequently the centre of poltergeist activity.

One other element in many poltergeist cases is psychological: an element of frustration, whether due to environment or attitude, is often found. Dr George Owen, then of Cambridge University and now of Toronto, visited Sauchie and featured the case in his excellent book *Can We Explain the Poltergeist?*. He writes of Virginia's arrival in Sauchie from rural Ireland.

> In effect she lost her father, her mother, her dog, her only intimate friend and her familiar surroundings. From the status of an only child she became one of three. She had to share a bed with Margaret. With the best will in the world on all sides, this can be acutely distressing, especially for a girl in her stage of development. The vehemence of the poltergeist when it was proposed that Margaret return to the bed may be significant.

Nonetheless while frustration may be a factor it takes us no nearer an explanation of what *kind* of force is at work. Certainly many of the activities of the poltergeist fit in with the personality of a frustrated child: throwing things through windows; rappings which seem to demand attention; and increased fervour when the subject is rendered passive by being put to bed. This has led many people to suggest that the children are "faking". Undoubtedly this does happen, especially when they learn that it makes them a centre of attention or that the investigators may well go away without witnessing anything and they want to "help things along".

Most investigators have encountered such pranks and the general comment is that "you soon learn to distinguish the real phenomena from false ones". Equally, some of the events could not be faked: there are too many witnesses who will testify otherwise. Dr Owen writes: "In my opinion the Sauchie case must be regarded as establishing beyond all reasonable doubt the objective reality of some poltergeist phenomena."

Happily, poltergeists usually have a shortish life of a few months, then disappear for good. This is fortunate for the families concerned, who often suffer severe distress. With experienced help they can be guided through the situation and have their fears reduced in proportion. In Virginia's case her schoolmates showed great understanding and, according to Miss Stewart, protected her from marauding journalists. (In the Springburn case which I shall describe shortly, the boys were subjected to jeers and persecuted by their school-fellows.) The Sauchie poltergeist made its exit in April 1961, about five months after it had begun. It had abated briefly in the preceding December, following a service of intercession conducted by the Rev. Professor Murdo Ewen McDonald, then minister of St George's West in Edinburgh. (The Church of Scotland has never practised the exorcism of persons and has now declared that blessing and healing procedures are sufficient.)

Professor McDonald was also involved in the second case, which occurred in 1974 in Springburn in Glasgow. This poltergeist made Sauchie look mild in comparison. It lasted a year and ran through the gamut of poltergeist activity. The principal investigators on this occasion were Astronomy Professor Archie Roy of Glasgow University, who is an SPR member, and the Rev. Max Magee, who was then Chaplain at

Strathclyde University and Secretary of the Church of Scotland Working Party on Parapsychology.

The Grieve family lived in the Springburn area of Glasgow. Years afterwards, they are still reluctant to speak about the case and claim to have suffered much from the way neighbours reacted to them. Indeed the case first came to a head because of a complaint by their immediate neighbours. Both families occupied a semi-detached council house with aluminium/steel walls, of the type which were put up rapidly around the perimeter of many cities after the war. Mr Grieve described the sequence of events on Sunday, 3 November, 1974, at 10.00 p.m., as follows:

> It is the nightly routine of my wife and I to enter our sons' bedroom to say goodnight. Their ages are fourteen and eleven years. Shortly after, the two boys came into the lounge to tell us they heard tapping noises coming from the wall behind their headboards. We went into their bedroom and heard for ourselves those mysterious bangings on the wall. Then tappings seemed to be coming from under the beds. A few minutes later another sound was added. That was a strange 'scratching' which sounded like fingernails being drawn down a piece of wood. This went on and on until 6 a.m. on November 4th.
>
> Hoping that there may be some reasonable explanation for these weird noises, we continued to witness the same experience night after night every time our sons tried to lie down to sleep. However, when we discovered that this was an unending nightmare, we moved the boys into our own bedroom only to find that these horrible noises had followed us. Every night after that we continued to call the Police Authorities who actually witnessed all of these sounds, themselves. Our other witnesses included a 'police officer', a well known 'Baillie'', a recently appointed 'councillor' and some neighbours.

But the empty house beneath was soon to be occupied by a family named Keenan. They believed the Grieves were causing the noises and refused to accept the assurance of Inspector Hackson, of the Marine Division of Glasgow Police, that this was not the case. Throughout the coming days, as the noises got louder and more frequent, relations between the two families were broken off. Then came a more sinister development.

17

Once more the following night we tried again to put our sons into their own beds, and as usual within minutes the 'bangings and tappings' and 'scratchings' resumed, then rapid tappings followed by the rhythm of the "Dead March". Being a musician, my wife, and our younger son Jeffrey (who is also learning music), immediately recognised the beat, my wife thinking that someone was trying to play a rather 'sick' practical joke, asked out loud "Who are you", again the beat (under the bed) of the "Dead March" was played out by tapping.

It was from this moment onwards that we were aware that something unnatural was really happening. The problem was how could we decipher these tappings. Then a very simple method of using this occurred to my wife. If answer to a definite question was No, our mysterious 'guest' would knock once, if the answer was Yes, there would be two knocks. If a message or sentence was to be related to us my wife said she would go through the alphabet slowly and each letter which was to be significant would receive two knocks. Through this very slow and tiring method the message which was received informed us of a "pit disaster" which happened (in this immediate area) many years ago, and resulted in the deaths of some miners, and our ghost went on to tell us that they couldn't find rest and wanted to find peace through the efforts of our family.

As a method of coherent communication, Yes/No questions are very misleading. Put alongside that, the fact is that "mischievous" poltergeists are often perverse and sometimes exhibit a kind of petulant intelligence designed to mislead investigators. When addressed aloud, for instance, the poltergeist sometimes replies with machine-gun raps or throws something at the questioner. Similarly, most poltergeist experts would be sceptical about accepting the idea of "unquiet souls" as the cause of the phenomena. Poltergeists rarely give coherent information in the way that a medium's "control" does and seem to owe much of their "personality" to a projected or acquired element, dependent on the focus or their surroundings.

The Grieves, however, did call in various Spiritualist mediums. By this time the bangs had been going on for four weeks and despite several seances and blessing services, the phenomena continued. Water dripped from the ceiling and pools of water were found on the floor. A tap was broken off and the bathroom flooded. Ash-trays, clocks and table lamps were all thrown around the room in front of witnesses. Max Magee made tape-recordings of the bangs and scratching noises which were coming from the walls. These were so loud that it sounded as if a sledgehammer was being wielded, but on touring the interior and exterior of the house while the recorder was running he could discover no physical cause. A plumber was called and tightened the bathroom tap with a wrench. He had only been gone an hour when the taps apparently turned themselves on and locked in the open position. So he had to be called again. This time he had to use both hands on his wrench to turn the tap off.

Mrs Grieve's mother, Mrs Anderson, who is the householder of the flat in Springburn, got up one evening to go out of the lounge. The chair she had been sitting on rose several feet in the air, travelled across the room and crashed to the ground. Mrs Anderson collapsed with shock. During this period, the investigators spent many nights sleeping on the floor, monitoring the activities. No one could claim that the Grieves were gaining anything by fraud. Mrs Grieve and her mother were nervous wrecks. Mrs Grieve had hardly any sleep and the boys were subject to jeers and ostracism at school. The family managed to avoid publicity (except for a couple of short newspaper stories) and went ex-directory with their telephone.

Throughout all of this the finger pointed at the two boys as the focus of activity. In an attempt to escape from the house, the family moved in with relatives named Brouwer who lived nearby. This worked to some extent but some of the phenomena, such as object movements, occurred in the Brouwer household. Curiously very little happened when the boys were at school and the activity began when they returned and were together. But the explanation that they were a dual "focus" took a knock when Jeffrey, the younger boy, went on holiday in the North of Scotland with his granny, Mrs Anderson. A piece of metal hit the boy on the forehead without anyone near and Mrs Anderson found that jewellery in a drawer had been "apported" elsewhere. The idea that the boy was deliberately playing tricks on his grandmother was not accepted by the investigators. Dereck also went on holiday, with friends of the family, to Spain: there, a shaving mirror

19

hung on a tent pole drifted out a foot in a horizontal direction and dropped to the ground. The family friend, who until then had been sceptical about the poltergeist, was watching and was now convinced. The next day, while they were lying on towels at the beach, sand spurted up in jets all around them.

The phenomena appeared to concentrate where the boys were present, but one day when the family were out of the house, one of the strangest events occurred. They returned to find that cushions from the armchairs in the lounge had been substituted for drawers in the sideboard. The drawers were sitting in place of the cushions. The poltergeist also showed its ingenuity in teleporting a mirror from the hallway through the closed door of the lounge and through the closed door of the kitchen, where a crash brought the family running to discover what had happened. A "gonk" doll which sat on the television set, hopped from the room and apparently was able to dematerialise and rematerialise at will. It would often spin round like an animated cartoon while the family were watching television. The boys also levitated from their beds a few feet into the air while being watched by Professor Roy and Max Magee. Unfortunately no photographs were taken of this and, even if they had been, people who were not present at the time might be inclined to suggest that they were "trampolining" in a playful style. Professor Roy is sure that they were not. He finds amazing similarities between the Springburn poltergeist and the one at Enfield in Essex in 1977-8, during which photographs were taken of the girls in mid-flight across their bedroom.

The Springburn case ought to rank as one of the "classics", but at the time of the events the main concern of Max Magee and Professor Roy was to bring peace and normality back to the Grieve house, which was a friendly and harmonious home with no record of psychiatric disturbance. Both boys were examined by Dundee psychiatrist, Dr James McHarg, a member of the Society for Psychical Research and well acquainted with psychic phenomena. They were found to be normal. Certainly, Dereck Grieve was experiencing frustration at his failed attempts to obtain an apprenticeship and the phenomena did cease about the time when he obtained a job as an apprentice electrician in the city centre store where his father worked. But if this is the cause, poltergeists of such dimensions ought to be found among Glasgow's unemployed youth in abundance. The younger boy lost six months at school throughout the episode and the family suffered a great deal by it individually and collectively. Even allowing for the possibility that the observers were duped by a clever conspiracy involving the whole family, a motive for trickery has still to be produced.

Yet poltergeist phenomena remain highly controversial. As one authority has pointed out: "Antagonists of psi [general term for extra-sensory activity] regard them as the peak of superstitious beliefs." The author of those words is Professor Hans Bender, Director of Freiburg Institute, who was closely involved with a case which was to change public opinion largely because it was documented on film. Although he has investigated some thirty-five poltergeists since the last war, Professor Bender gives the Rosenheim case pride of place.

In November 1967, in the Bavarian town of Rosenheim, inexplicable events were happening in a lawyer's office. These appeared to centre on a secretary named Annemarie Sch——. There were fluctuations in the power supply, fuses were blown, bulbs exploded or were unscrewed from their sockets. Fluid in copy machines was spilled inexplicably and sharp bangs were reported. Four telephones would ring simultaneously and telephone bills reached unbelievable figures. A meter installed by the post office traced innumerable calls to the number 0119, the speaking clock. It takes at least seventeen seconds to dial and connect with this number, yet it was being dialled four or five, even six times per minute, for minutes on end.

Eventually one researcher spotted lamps in a corridor swinging as Annemarie, a nineteen-year-old secretary, walked past. By then fresh disturbances, which were much like the traditional PK (psychokinetic) effects, began. Filing cabinets shunted around. Pictures flew through the air. Annemarie was sent away and the disturbances stopped. She went ten-pin bowling and all the scoring equipment went haywire. When she came back to work and the disturbances started again, she was sacked. She found other jobs but her fiance said that in the circumstances their marriage was impossible. Life was not easy for Annemarie.

21

Once I was working in Regenfelchen at a paper mill and there was an accident and a man was killed. The other workers had all heard about me and they said, "This woman is responsible for that man's death!" They didn't sack me but it didn't take me long to get the message, so I left.

Years ago Annemarie would have been burned as a witch. Professor Bender adopted milder methods. He put her through psychological tests and found that there were inner frustrations, partly sexual, and an unstable personality structure. But this was not excessive: she is now happily married with three children and there is apparently no sign of poltergeist activity reappearing. What her case did do was to demonstrate through television that careful documentation of the evidence makes it difficult for the sceptic to deny that poltergeists are for real.

Those three cases are all well attested by witnesses and in addition to reading the accounts I have spoken to several reliable witnesses in the Sauchie and Springburn cases. The fourth case I saw for myself in 1978 during the making of a BBC Scotland television programme, on which I acted as reporter and for which we shot some unique film. Not only is this case extraordinary for the "voices" which were a feature, but the investigators claim that because of their own detailed documentation it will rank as the "poltergeist of all time".

At Enfield, Essex, in September 1977, the SPR investigators had been called by the *Daily Mirror* after they were phoned by a Mrs Hodgson of 284 Green Street in Ponders End. The SPR contingent was considerable. Maurice Grosse, an inventor of vending machines, brought his cassette recorder. Guy Lyon Playfair, an author, brought his experience of Brazilian poltergeists. In their wake were speech therapists, dental surgeons, video tape operators and various other psychic researchers with experience of poltergeist phenomena, known to the professionals as RSPK (Recurrent Spontaneous Psychokinesis). Quietly observing in the corner of the room on a number of evenings was Graham Morris, a freelance photographer whose patience was rewarded with photographs of a Lego brick flying through the air and of the children levitating. Grosse and Playfair displayed great diligence, the latter paying more than fifty visits and Grosse clocking up about a thousand hours on the case.

At the centre of all this attention were two girls — Margaret, aged thirteen, and Janet, aged eleven. Together with their two younger brothers, they lived with their mother, a forty-seven-year-old lady with a heart big enough to play host to all these visitors without complaining, despite the fact that she suffered from a bronchial complaint and had been through a divorce from a husband with a history of schizophrenia. Mrs Hodgson's brother, Mr John Birkham, lived nearby with his wife, Sylvia, at 272 Green Street. Next door lived Vic and Peggy Nottingham, an attractive couple in their forties. They first became aware of the knockings in September 1977. The police were called and WPC Carolyn Heeps gave this account of her first visit along with PC Ayres.

> . . . PC Ayres and some neighbours went into the kitchen and they tested all the pipes, tapped the pipes, the walls, opened up the refrigerator to see if any of the noises there would cause it, and what I noticed, was in the living room. It was still in darkness. One of the elder boys of the family came up to me and said, "Look at the chair". The chair was by the sofa, and I looked at the chair, and I noticed it shook slightly, I can't explain it any better, and it came off the floor, oh, nearly a half inch I should say, and I saw it slide off to the right about three and a half to four feet before it came to rest. I checked to see whether or not it could have slid along the floor. I placed a marble on the floor to see if the marble would go in the same direction as the chair did, and it didn't. It didn't roll at all. I checked for wires under the cushions of the chair, and I could find no explanation at all. I'm absolutely convinced that no one in that room touched that chair or went anywhere near it when it moved. Absolutely convinced.

Over the next two months the phenomena increased in variety and number. Maurice Grosse's own catalogue of varieties of phenomena, observed personally or from signed or taped statements of third parties involved, includes the following:

> *Psychokinetic*—knocking, rapid transit of small objects, lateral and vertical movement of furniture including a settee, chairs, tables, dressing table, beds, chest of drawers, and articles such as table lamps, kitchen utensils, books, cushions, toys etc. Doors opening and

23

closing, lights switching on and off, and interference with electrical and mechanical apparatus.

Apports—coins, book, teapots, water, tea bags, plastic etc.

Apparitions—various. Experienced by mother, both daughters, niece, neighbour. Two apparitions seen were of myself.

Light Phenomena—a glowing light on the stairs seen by the uncle and a green circular floating light seen by *Daily Mirror* photographer.

Voice Phenomena—voice emanating from three children and Raudive (High Frequency) voices and sounds heard directly on tape.

Psychological or Parapsychological Activity—trance states and audible shared dreams.

Other Phenomena—cold draughts, offensive smells, physical contact of 'presence', automatic writing in sleep, pushing, tickling, pinching, all apparently paranormally activated.

The apparitions witnessed by the family were of a middle-aged man smoking a cigarette in an upstairs bedroom and of Mr Grosse drawing the downstairs curtains and ignoring a neighbour at the door. (It was established that he was actually upstairs at the time.)

But the most controversial aspect of the Enfield poltergeist is the "voice". This deep, throaty sound came from both girls but mostly from Janet. During its speech the girls' lips hardly moved at all. It resembled a growl and rose to the quality of a loud bark at times. The "voices" had names (Andrew Gardiner and Stewart Sertint) and later acquired the ability to speak. Young Billy, aged six, took to emulating his sisters with a "voice" calling itself "Dirty Dick". An echo from "The Exorcist", and possible emulation cannot be ruled out but whether this would be a similar phenomenon, the girls copying the film or the poltergeist copying the film, I am not sure. Often the Voice would conduct rapid staccato conversations for hours without apparently harming the girls' vocal chords. They were tested by a laryngograph supplied by Professor Adrian Foursin of the Department of Phonetics at University College, London. He examined the trace brought back (it is a graphic record of muscle responses in the voice box in the way that an EEG measures heart activity) and concluded that the girls' normal voice was typical for girls of their age, whereas the Voice was using the false vocal chords, a phenomenon known as pico-ventricularis. But, added the Professor, "the girls were doing something that most kids could do if they played around with voice quality." He preferred to use Occam's Razor to cut the Voice's throat — the simplest explanation, in the absence of better alternatives, was that the girls were having a good game. "Why does the external agency go to so much trouble to use the false vocal chords when the ordinary ones would be equally usable and give clearer communication?" The question is fair but, as we have seen, the logic of a poltergeist does not work to a higher rationale. If the girls are ventriloquising then they are very good at it, keeping their lips closed and keeping up repartee with the spectators.

The *Daily Mirror* sent ventriloquist Ray Allan along and he is alleged to have extracted a "confession" from Margaret that she was creating the Voice. But the next day she told Grosse that she had thought he was asking her about Easter holidays and had nodded her head, which was interpreted as an admission. We must also beware of attaching too much weight to a child's confession — often it takes place under strain caused by the phenomena and a desire to be free of the trial. Both girls are lovable and neither is severely disturbed. They do enjoy the attention they get (Janet even mischievously) but it is difficult to believe that they could have mounted a cleverly orchestrated attempt to create all the phenomena. Perhaps they were tempted to mimic the Voice. But pull chairs around with hidden wires? Project Lego bricks with the fast and unusual trajectories which accompany poltergeist activity? Produce loud bangs like a sledgehammer hitting the wall, and acquire the ability to leap feet in the air without being caught faking? Maurice Grosse has a stiff answer for the doubters.

If anybody goes away from this case and says it's a fake then you accuse at least twenty ordinary good people of being either charlatans or liars and for what reason? For what reason do people like myself — I've my own business to run — spend God only knows how many nights down here?

The Second International Conference of the Society for Psychical Research, held at Trinity College, Cambridge, in March 1978, heard a symposium on the case given by Grosse and Playfair. Video-cassettes of the Voice case were shown and much debate ensued. Some were sceptical about the authenticity of the voices and appeared to imply that all the phenomena were therefore suspect. Playfair hit back: "Some people in this society [SPR] seem to deny there's such a thing as a poltergeist; well, if you do so in the face of all this evidence you shouldn't be a member." Other experienced researchers felt that Grosse and Playfair had given equal weight to all the phenomena or perhaps too much to the Voice, when they should have discriminated between genuine events and attention-arresting devices on the part of the children. They concluded that in the emotional disturbance resulting from the loss of their father they had a motive for producing the poltergeist tricks to gain attention. But this argument can be countered. First, there has been no financial gain by the family, who are poor; second, even if Janet wanted it to continue, the others showed signs of weariness and the phenomena are such that Janet alone could not have produced them all. We are faced with postulating a conspiracy on behalf of the whole Hodgson family (probably the neighbours too) who, I am certain, are incapable of the sleight of hand and ingenuity which professional conjurers might possess. The only other explanation is that Grosse and Playfair are staging the poltergeist hoax of all time with the Hodgsons as accomplices. While their ready agreement to co-operate with news media covering the case may be criticised by some SPR members, I believe it clears them of any charge of manipulating evidence. Throughout the case they offered every facility to investigators to see for themselves.

In the Rosenheim case it was important to establish film evidence for the authenticity of RSPK. At Enfield, Graham Morris' photographs, taken in the girls' bedroom, show the girls levitating — there is a sixth of a second between the exposures, the first of which was triggered by sound monitoring the girls' bedroom and listening for any potential action. Maurice Grosse's tapes are weighty evidence. Even if you dismiss the Voice, the taps and bangs are of a quality which cannot be reproduced by hitting the walls of the house.

During the filming at Enfield, I was interviewing the two girls, who were talking in the Voice from time to time. The whole family vere under observation when the following sequence took place on film:

Janet:	Yea, it slung a cupboard at Mum, it hit Mum; it slung a book shelf at Margaret here.
Stewart Lamont:	Have you tried telling it to go away?
Margaret:	Yes, many times.
Janet:	No answer, nothing.
Stewart L.:	What does it reply?
Janet:	No it won't, it'll stay another six or seven years.
Stewart L.:	What about the voices, when did the voices start?
Janet:	December the 12th.
Stewart L.:	And how did they start?
Janet:	Well, one night Mr Grosse was talking about it. About eight-thirty, he said, what we need now is the voices to talk. And that night we went to bed, and I can't remember exactly what happened . . . [*three loud knocks*] . . . and . . .
Stewart L.:	What's that knocking?
Janet:	Yea.
Margaret:	That's . . . you can hear it now, it was doing that yesterday morning and Peggy was on h r own, so she come into us because it wasn't her. She come in, and we sat together and we heard it. And I counted how many knocks and there was fourteen altogether and it's doing it again now.
Stewart L.:	That was three knocks just now.
Margaret:	Yes, it goes in threes and twos.
Janet:	When we first got contact, this was when Mr Grosse said if there's anyone there, knock twice for yes, and if not, one for no.
Stewart L.:	I wonder if we did that now whether it would answer? Is anybody there? [*silence*] Is anybody there? [*silence*] Nothing.
Girls:	No.
Janet:	It doesn't always do it to order.
Margaret:	No, it goes in spasms. Like, we're talking now, it may knock now after you've said that, but it won't do it when you want it to straight away you know.

27

There is no doubt in my mind that what the film recorded was poltergeist activity. I remain open-minded about the Voices. There are nonetheless strong reasons for not excluding them from the list of evidence, which is considerable. It is all too easy to pay one visit to the Hodgson home, as some have done, and conclude that the Voices are ventriloquised. But they are able to keep up conversations for hours without any apparent soreness in the girls' throats. Janet and Margaret say the Voices seem to come from the back of their heads and are involuntary. They utter obscenities, which is not a facet of the girls' normal behaviour. When cross-examined roughly, they seem to get sharper and more impudent in reply. Could they be some form of dissociated personality which is being made use of by the poltergeist? Grosse and Playfair have encouraged the Voices in an attempt to find whether there is an entity behind the poltergeist, and they suspect it might be linked with a murder nearby. They also say that when prayer and God are mentioned there is a hostile reaction. However, this is not to say that "possession" is taking place. There is no question of taking over the girls or of malevolence in the Voice. Fear has never been allowed to get an upper hand, perhaps because of the calming attitude of the researcher. This is an important fact in any "possession" or poltergeist, which seems to be not so much an independent personality, but one which draws strength and characteristics from the weaknesses of the focus or subject.

The Enfield poltergeist has now died down. The girls were taken into care temporarily when their mother's health finally broke down. That is a sad footnote to what must have been a paralysing experience for the family. Although the girls seemed to enjoy the attention it brought them and perhaps even "helped things along" on occasions, there is no doubt in my mind that most of the phenomena could not be and was not conjured by them.

But what can be said to explain these four cases? Is there any theory as to what constitutes a poltergeist or what makes RSPK work? There are in fact several and the simplest is that the phenomena are the result of childish pranks: that is, not to put too fine a point on it, *fraud and trickery*. The motive usually advanced is that this is consonant with adolescent behaviour and compounded where there is an element of frustration

28

present. It exploits tension. It gains and arrests attention. This argument does not apply to the four cases outlined here because it ignores several factors. In the first place, as well as arresting attention, the phenomena caused great (sometimes lasting) distress to the family and to the "focus". Hardly a wilful gain. Secondly, the corroborative testimony of a number of witnesses rules out the possibility of fraud in all four cases. Thirdly, the children involved would have to exercise great ingenuity with wires, sleight of hand and so on to fool all of these people all of the time. They would have to be geniuses of illusion. Finally, there are various parallels and coincidences between the four cases.

The last reason is to my mind the most weighty in favour of authenticity. The symptoms of a rare disease, when found in several patients, allow a diagnosis to be built up from the common characteristics. If fraud were at work, it presupposes that the focus has mugged up on all the poltergeist literature in order to reproduce the full gamut of phenomena. Yet the Campbell girl, the Grieve boys and the Hodgson girls did not know what a poltergeist was until it hit them (literally). When it did hit them, it did so in its own peculiar way. Objects would fly across the room curving, not following the parabolic path of an object under the earth's gravitational field. This unusual trajectory is not easy to reproduce, far less be aware of, unless you have read up the details of poltergeist behaviour.

Another explanation is that many of the events were caused by HALLUCINATIONS on the part of those present. Besides involving the rare idea of group hallucination, this theory demands that these took place with different groups on different occasions. Even more far-fetched is the suggestion that the children hypnotised the researchers, planting the hallucinations in their minds. The final nail in the coffin of this theory is the tape and film evidence. The camera does not hallucinate.

Yet another theory was advanced by G. W. Lambert in 1955 and has had a good innings. It is the so-called GEOPHYSICAL theory which looks for explanations of the noises and movements associated with RSPK in terms of soil mechanics, seismic disturbances and house construction stresses. Quite apart from the fact that it offers no explanation for such things as Stigmata (marks on flesh) or Fireraising or Apports (and hence is deficient as a theory), it does not explain why only one house is a target. If subsidence of underground tunnels or an earthquake were at work we would expect this to affect a whole neighbourhood. In any case, the force required to reproduce the bangs of a poltergeist or the vibrational energy necessary to move a teacup off a mantelpiece by this means is considerable, as A. Cornell and A. G. Gauld calculated in 1961. Subsequently they performed experiments on a row of houses in Cambridge, swinging 18 lb. weights against the walls from up to twenty feet away. They failed to dislodge a teacup sitting on a mantelpiece on the other side of the wall. Using a low frequency vibrator cemented into a wall, they found that they needed a 1,600 lb. thrust before things started to vibrate within the rooms. Before the teacup would take off, it would have required a thrust sufficient to demolish the house! They decided not to go this far and lived to tell the tale. In the three British poltergeist cases discussed previously, geophysical explanations were checked and eliminated. So the geophysical theory bites the dust.

One fact which emerged in that study was the magnitude of the physical forces apparently at work in RSPK. The PSYCHON theory involves some form of energy extruding from the "focus" and performing the feats. "Action at a distance" might be possible if the focus channelled energy either from some "anima mundi/group mind" or did so via "ectoplasm" (as spiritualist mediums allegedly do). Or there might be some kind of field force at work which is not gravitational or electromagnetic but produces similar effects. This would differ from other field theory. In science a field cannot be selective (taking one flower from a vase and leaving the rest, for example), thus this theory demands that we postulate a new force which cannot be measured or tested. Until it can this issue must remain simply a speculation.

PSYCHONEUROTIC theories have also been advanced. As Owen points out, with a single exception, overt psychosis is absent from poltergeist cases but psychoneurotic conditions are reported with a relatively higher incidence than in the general population. He suggests that anxiety is often a precipitating factor, giving rise to cerebral activity which releases abnormal powers. The incidence among pubescents may suggest that there is also something of a physiological basis. The fact that this is not always the case suggests that the association with adolescence is probably more likely to be psychological than physiological. The physical symptoms would then be explained as a "conversion symptom" — the cork which pops off the beer bottle as the invisible gas pressure increases due to fermentation. In this process there is a secondary neurotic gain of attention-seeking. Hormonal changes and sublimated sexual energy may seem plausible as factors in the process. Indeed the incidence of RSPK among adolescents (and more often than not, a pubescent girl) may be significant. The fact that cure by hypnosis has been effected in some cases would again point to a psychological cause. Sleep appears to inhibit the poltergeist whose activity often reaches a peak when the child-focus goes to bed. This seems to link it to consciousness. Further factors which link RSPK to human consciousness are that it appears to affect humans and not animals, and that it appears to attach to a person more often than a place. Yet, like many aspects of the poltergeist, these statements are not without exceptions. Sir William Barrett, one of the patriarchs of psychical research, identified nine aspects, some of which have already been mentioned. The others again point to some mental or psychological basis for RSPK, viz:

> The phenomena are temporary and sporadic and fade away like a virus infection; and they produce annoyance but rarely injury.
>
> There is apparent intelligence behind many poltergeist actions.
>
> The poltergiest is apparently inhibited by suggestion.

Thus we may conclude that the poltergeist is not "geist", but somehow related to, or a product of, the Human Mind.

Another German word which suggests this is a form of the GESTALT theory. This theory affirms the existence of realities which are not just the sum of component parts: for instance, melody is more than just a collection of musical notes. Hence in this form of theory, a poltergeist may be some kind of entity with meaning, inasmuch as it is related to human consciousness and not just a collection of happenings. It appears to select "objects" to move or apport. Yet these objects have no existence in the world of particle physics as watches or teacups — they are simply collections of atoms and molecules in the shape of something which needs human consciousness to recognise it in this Gestalt. If the poltergeist is not an intelligent force, why does it select a whole watch and not five-eighths of it to "apport"? Similarly, the poltergeist seems to recognise the territorial gestalt of one house and not another. To a non-intelligent RSPK, this ought to appear simply as a random collection of bricks and mortar. Both these theories — Psychoneurotic and Gestalt — are attractive and seem to fit in with many of the observed characteristics of RSPK. However, although they point to *why* it might be going on (I.e. the *nature* of RSPK) they cannot explain *how* it takes place.

The final theory is the MEDIUMISTIC one. Either the focus acts as a trigger for an entity known as a poltergeist to come into operation; or the focus is the medium through which discarnate and unquiet spirits create the RSPK effects; or aspects of the medium are dissociated as in the Psychon theory. Support for the second alternative is often forth-coming because many people jump to the conclusion that paranormal events are linked with "evil spirits". Of the three cases which I examined, it was significant that in all three, such explanations were advanced at some point. In Sauchie someone uncovered the fact that, in 1696, a Christian Shaw was the victim of witchcraft. In Springburn, the mine disaster story was elicited by the family in response to raps on the table. In Enfield, a man had murdered his wife nearby. To all this the sceptic will reply that there is not a spot in the country that does not have some "dirty deed" connected with it if you dig far enough in history. I would heartily agree, for once this fact is revealed, the capacity of the poltergeist to respond to suggestion and its ability to make mischief out of it, renders it very difficult to test. As we shall see in the chapter on Survival, all that glitters is not gold and all that speaks from beyond the grave is not dead.

There is also a great difference between a poltergeist and what takes place at a seance. Seance mediumship is more coherent and the medium can acquire conscious control over its content or else sinks into trance. Neither of these things happens in RSPK which do not need (and indeed often resist) the medium/focus there for them to happen. The spiritualist sometimes explains RSPK as the result of "earthbound spirits" which are unable to progress, creating a nuisance because they are the vandals and delinquents of the spirit world. They cite the "voice" communication as evidence that there is intelligence at work, and would also argue that its coherent character is the result of the inexperience of the medium. This does not explain why the focus does not grow in these abilities over the months of the poltergeist's life instead of apparently losing the gift. Possibly there is some physiological factor (puberty?) which enables the tuner/amplifier of the focus to be better attuned. But for every RSPK which gives evidence of a "spirit" behind it, there are others which are "mindless" and do not appear to have any intelligent purpose.

Haunting, which is often accompanied by Apparitions and Auditory phenomena, may at first sight seem to be the same thing as a poltergeist. But there are several differences. First, the haunt occurs perhaps once or twice and these are perhaps separated by years, whereas the poltergeist has intense activity for a short period, ranging from days to six years (the longest to date, although the average is about three months). Second, it is connected with a place and not with a person as the RSPK so often are. Apparently it is often tied to some past event or person, not to a set of conditions in the present. Also it can be triggered off by a number of people and does not have a focus.

Nonetheless, an incident in the life of the Victorian super-psychic, D. D. Home, is worthy of mention. It was related in 1964 by Mr Hector McNeill, the grandson of a cousin of Home. The two men had been calling on a mutual friend in a set of farm cottages near Currie in Midlothian. He claimed that his tenant in the cottage next door refused to pay his rent and Home undertook to "spook" him out. Going into trance, not a few minutes elapsed before the tenant emerged from his cottage in a fearful state, claiming that his house was haunted. Chairs and tables had been shunting around, fire irons had been dancing on the hearth. He declared he was leaving, to the delight of Home, who was bathed in sweat from his efforts. Thus was there a poltergeist produced to order! Lacking in corroboration as this tale is, it is not worth offering as evidence, but it does remind us that Mediumship and Poltergeists are not totally unrelated. The superpsychic of the seventies, Mathew Manning, started his psychic career as the focus of a poltergeist. George Owen has suggested that "poltergeistery and physical mediumship are essentially manifestations of the same thing". Physical mediumship (such as producing apports, moving objects or levitating) is rare and it is doubtful whether a medium should be encouraged to produce an anti-social creature like a poltergeist. But at the moment there does not appear to be anyone who can harness the energy of a poltergeist — and this is considerable, as evidence the moving of large objects. We are driven back to one of the theories to explain what is happening and the moment we think we have captured the genie in our bottle, it has popped up elsewhere with new tricks which confound the previous theory.

Perhaps all that can be said in conclusion is that a poltergeist enjoys breaking his own rules as well as other people's furniture. He appears to need human company, especially that of adolescents, but doesn't have a huge life-span. While he exists, he creates havoc in a home — and in our understanding of Mind and Matter.

Chapter 2

All in the Mind?—Apparitions

Apparition . . . ghost . . . haunting. The words have a melodramatic ring. The associations which spring to mind are of headless cavaliers riding to their doom or of stately homes and castles haunted by suicides and jilted lovers. But the odds are that the event known as a haunting or an apparition as often as not happens in a council house and the ghostly figure is liable to be someone quite unremarkable. Apparitions can be of many kinds. They can be of living or dead persons; they can be solid or ethereal in appearance; they can be of animals or inanimate objects; they can appear purposefully or be meaningless; they are more often benevolent than malevolent. They can be seen by several persons at once or only be seen by one person among a group. Sometimes they speak and are even tangible; at other times they are detached and are identified by a sense of presence and a chill atmosphere. In short, ghosts have many guises and, judging from statistics available, one in eight people will see one at some point in their lives and of every three witnesses, two will be women.

The industry of what I shall call "classic" ghost stories is a busy and indeed a growing one. Self-appointed ghost hunters and societies are growing up everywhere and advertising for experiences. There are books on haunted castles and houses, books on theatrical ghosts and on ghost armies fighting battles. What is intriguing about them is that often the "true" stories seem every bit as gripping as fictional tales published under the banner of "horror" stories.

But the temptation to write gripping yarns of the supernatural does not always do justice to the facts — if there are any. It is frustrating, but all too common, when investigating the basis of a classic ghost story, that the nearer you come to the original testimony, the more vague it becomes. Or else the story begins to lose some of its imaginative detail. The mirage dissolves on close inspection. Why then do such stories persist if they have little basis in fact? Often the motive is to keep alive a tourist myth. Typical of such tales is that of the ghost of Glamis Castle in Angus (family home of the Queen Mother) in which it is said there is a secret chamber used by a previous Earl to hide a deformed progeny which was half-man, half-monster. A century ago, white cloths were hung from all the windows by curious guests and, assembling on the castle lawn, they spied some rooms without the white markers. The outraged Earl returned before they had a chance to investigate and sent the house party packing. In writing about the Glamis legend, the *Daily Telegraph Magazine* adopted a credulous and all-too-easy approach; they couldn't find the answer so they concluded it must be a mystery. . . .

> For 150 years this monster lived in the castle, only emerging to crawl about at night. The secret, by custom of the family, is known only to the Earl and his heir. The present Earl says he was never told, though he is certain that the chamber exists, somewhere. According to Lord Halifax, whose Ghost book includes a chapter on Glamis, knowledge of the secret had a depressing affect on all who were told it. After a while the custom lapsed, though the mystery persists and the monster may still lurk in the walls. . . .

And pigs may still fly. Notice how all the evidence had disappeared but much is made of the Earl's certainty that "something . . . somewhere . . .". In fact when I contacted the Castle authorities the most they would claim was that there was possibly a dummy chamber but none was known and neither the Factor nor the Earl knew of any substantial evidence for anything paranormal. Understandably, the Factor declines any offer to hang hankerchiefs out of the windows and doesn't go out of his way to bury the ghost of the monster. I am sure it helps the tourists to capture something of the "Macbeth" atmosphere.

Before he began seeing apparitions, Macbeth was Thane of

Glamis. He was also Thane of Fife and in that ancient Kingdom, nestling in a picturesque bay, lies the "Auld Grey Toun" of St Andrews, for long the ecclesiastical capital of Scotland. It is also renowned for its university, its golf and — its ghosts. Within sight of the gaunt skeleton of St Andrews Cathedral, which still retains much of its grandeur, heretics were burned and two prelates were assassinated. A tourist can look out from the cliffs on which the Cathedral and its graveyard stand and turn back to prowl among the stones of the priory which once also stood on the site. Monks have been seen to walk the "Pends"; a white lady, buried in a tower-like tomb by the seaward wall of the Cathedral, and a nun who disfigured her face in a lovelorn agony are said to appear in this vicinity. Stories circulate that the last headmistress of St Leonard's School nearby (built on the site of the former St Leonard's College) had to change her bedroom because of a ghost. However, the lady in question cannot substantiate the story, nor can her successor. It seems somewhat killjoy to rip apart these romantic legends. But it is only if proper witnesses can attest written accounts of their experiences that any psychic fact can be given credence. I heard of a St Andrews businessman who saw a monk in the Pends in the winter of 1977. He wrote down an account at the time, but is fiercely shy of having it broadcast or published. This may well argue for the authenticity of his experience but it takes us no further in establishing the reality of paranormal phenomena among the ancient stones of St Andrews.

I did, however, encounter an Aberdeen spiritualist medium, Mr Russell Hunter, who had had a visionary experience in St Andrews Cathedral some years ago while on holiday. Standing in the ruined cloister, it changed before his eyes to its former ecclesiastical glory — monks were bustling to and fro. One of them who introduced himself as Brother John, beckoned him to follow but he held back as he had a strong impression that if he went after the monk he would not be able to return. (This kind of experience in which the whole environment changes to become part of the apparition has been called *metachoric*.)

Mr Hunter described a scene with Brother John clad in a black habit and student types in grey. There was a bustling trade on the slope from the Cathedral to the harbour (now a graveyard) and the monks seemed to be dealing with import-export business. Professor Donald Watt, who holds the Chair of Scottish Church History at St Andrews, confirms that the monks would have worn black and that contrary to expectation such trade would have been carried on even within Cathedral precincts. Some would argue that Mr Hunter's imagination created this scene, particularly because of the strong atmosphere of this historic place. Or was he, as a medium, capable of "triggering off" the whole sequence which was somehow stored in the stones in the way that a tape recorder retains audio signals? This experience was essentially subjective — it was not witnessed or recorded in any way. Not so a photograph taken by two ladies in another graveyard while they were compiling a book on gravestones. The photograph appeared to show the face of a lady wearing an old-fashioned pointed cap, which appeared on top of the headstone of a grave in the Greyfriars Kirkyard in Perth. Betty Willsher, who took the photograph, was once knocked off her bicycle by what she is certain was a supernatural entity while cycling up the Pends in St Andrews, ironically after attending a debate on whether ghosts exist, at which she voted for the negative!

The square tower which stands in the centre of the Cathedral grounds belongs to the ancient church of St Regulus. Robert de Montrose, the Prior of St Andrews, was said to have been thrown from its top after being knifed in the back by one of his monks who had been disciplined for playing fast-and-loose with women. More topically and tragically, a student committed suicide in 1978 by flinging himself from its parapet.

Access to the tower is by a very narrow stone stairway with a wider section, formerly of wood, near the bottom. On a summer day in 1948, a young actor from the Byre Theatre, Michael Elder, thought he would admire the view from the tower. Now known as a science-fiction writer, radio actor and "voice-over" for TV commercials, Elder recalls the incident vividly:

> I paid my threepence and was climbing the wooden stairs near the bottom when I noticed the legs of a man standing above me, clad in a sort of cassock. I didn't think of the strangeness of the dress at the time and when he asked if I was going up I said yes. "You can follow me up," he said, but when I got to the top and looked around, there

was no one in sight. There was no way that I could have squeezed past him on the narrow stair. I got a cold shiver, panicked and ran down the stairs as fast as I could. When I got out into the sunshine, the custodian was standing watching two men mowing the grass. I asked him if he had seen anyone come out of the tower. "There's been no one in or out since yourself," he replied.

Michael Elder is a credible witness and St Andrews is the kind of place you would *expect* to find ghosts. But I maintain that if they do exist, they ought also to be found in more modern settings. To be scientifically acceptable a phenomenon ought to be repeatable.

I thought I had found one such example which embodied all the thrilling aspects of the "classic" variety in the North-east of Scotland. It hadn't been written up, but was wide in circulation. The story goes that an Aberdeen lorry driver with the firm of Schlumberger had given a lift to a girl on a rainy night. He had dropped her at her house in Peterhead and gave her his anorak to keep her dry. He told her he would collect it when he returned by that route the next morning. However, when he called at the house the next day he thought that he must be mistaken because the young girl who lived there with her parents was not the same one. Then he saw a photograph on the mantelpiece — it was the girl who had borrowed his anorak. With dismay on their faces the couple told him that it was a photo of their daughter who had been killed two years ago. They offered to show him the grave, as he insisted that this girl had travelled in his cab. On reaching the graveyard, lying by the headstone . . . was his anorak.

Now, it should have been easy to find out which lorry driver was involved. But after much difficulty, one of the Schlumberger employees said that he knew the story and that he had known the girl. She was called Sheena B—— and he gave me the name of the street in Peterhead. I called on the Rev. James Miller, a minister friend who was then in Peterhead, and together we went to the local newspaper office, thinking that the matter ought to be approached with delicacy because of the sensibilities of the girl's parents, should the story prove to be false. The Editor apparently knew nothing but other staff at the office offered details which showed the story was well known locally. It was a taxi (not a lorry) which was involved and the girl Sheena B—— had been killed in a car accident about eight years previously on the Fraserburgh-Peterhead road, the spot at which she had been picked up. I went to see her father and was full of apologies when it appeared that the story was completely unfounded in fact. Only subsequently did I learn that the Editor phoned the manse to find out how "the lad from the BBC" had fared. During the conversation he revealed that he had discussed the story with Sheena B——'s father on several occasions; that he believed it himself; and he added the fact that the anorak was *green with a white cord*!

Just what should we make of that? You can lead a horse to water but you cannot make it drink. That proverb might well describe my reaction to obtaining evidence from the principal witnesses. It was not my job to persuade them to say this ghost existed, but to find out whether it did nor not. The North-east of Scotland and particularly that area known as Buchan is very hard-headed rural territory. It fosters a large membership of the notorious sect, the Close Brethren. But it is also a very superstitious area. Just down the coast from Peterhead there are a number of ghost stories around the spot where Bram Stoker sojourned while he was writing *Dracula*. I felt a little like the strangers who asked one of the Transylvanian locals to give an account of his legend.

However, even if that incident appears a waste of time and a waste of space in this book, it illustrates two things: how a ghost can become distorted and enlarged in the telling; and how sometimes witnesses will not talk about experiences, either for superstitious reasons or for fear of being thought soft in the head. And when supernatural stories become mixed with local culture they pass into the realm of legend.

This perhaps explains why the best-attested evidence for apparitions comes from urban areas where they do not acquire the currency of supernatural legends. This was the experience of Peter Moss, the historian and author, who was commissioned to write a book on contemporary ghosts. He advertised for experiences and was struck by the large number from Scotland, but significantly they were from the urban areas and not the Highlands. Expecting a large number of cranky replies, he was surprised by the normality of the people and the incidence of "ghost" experiences in very mundane situations. I was attracted to Peter Moss's book because it

40

contains sixty stories, mostly from the last decade. The age of the percipients ranged from twenty to eighty; the locations from council houses to a motorway toilet. Moss had also assembled his evidence in a highly readable form, but without the non-factual innuendo and credulity of the classic ghost books or stories in the tabloids about "things that go bump in the night". The book also had the advantage that many of the stories originated in Scotland, and names and addresses were easily obtainable to cross-check the witnesses' testimony. To Peter Moss's credit, all the witnesses I spoke to affirmed that he had conveyed their experience accurately.

The first incident I followed up involved someone whose profession deals constantly in the evaluation of evidence. Rosaleen Morrison is an Edinburgh advocate (or barrister in English terminology). In 1971 she stayed overnight with a hairdresser friend, Winston Hemmingsley, who was living with his girlfriend, Heather, in a flat in Red Lion Square, London. They had only recently moved into the flat and despite the fact that there was a spare room, they suggested that Rosaleen spend the night on a sofa in the lounge. Too tired to be bothered being kept up until they were ready to go to sleep, Rosaleen ascertained that the girl medical student who normally occupied the other room would not be returning that night and would not be requiring it. So she insisted on using the room. (She did not know at the time that the student would never require her room again, for she had committed suicide in it a few days earlier. Winston and Heather had helped clean up the blood which had spilled from her slashed wrists.) Soon asleep, Rosaleen was awakened by the sensation of someone's hair brushing her face.

Her immediate reaction in the confusion of waking was that Winston was attempting to seduce her, but his innocence was established when she recognised the young woman in the photograph on the mantelpiece, who now had long hair. Rosaleen knew at once that there must have been some mistake with dates and that the medical student returning late from a party, had come home to bed. "Who are you?" Rosaleen demanded instinctively.

The girl reached out to grab the bedclothes to pull them back and replied, "I'm Hilary, what are you doing in my bed?" Rosaleen felt that she must give some vindication of herself.

"Winston and Heather said I could stay here," she said. "It's only for one night. I'm very sorry."

"Oh, you mean there are others too," said Hilary, then sadly she added, "Oh dear," and straightening up, she moved to the door, apparently to discuss the matter with Winston.

Despite her embarrassment, Rosaleen Morrison was too sleepy to stay awake and it was only the next morning when she challenged Winston about Hilary's appearance that he blanched. Not only had he omitted to tell her about the suicide but he had not even mentioned Hilary's name to Rosaleen. He then realised that what she had seen was an apparition. I have confirmed the basic facts of this account with Winston Hemmingsley, who now has his own hairdresser's business in Glasgow, and with Rosaleen Morrison, who is the Belle of the Scottish Bar.

The second incident also involves an attractive woman. It is not that apparitions have predilections towards pretty ladies, but that women appear much more likely to encounter them than men, according to surveys which have been conducted. The lady involved on this occasion was Mrs Diane Samat of Garthdee, Aberdeen, who is remarkable among other things for the fact that she underwent a sterilisation operation following the break-up of her first marriage (of which there were three children), subsequently remarried, and amazingly was successful in having the operation reversed, having now had a baby with her new husband. Her experience of an apparition was in July 1976. Like Rosaleen Morrison it was not pleasant and it occurred while she was in bed. The figure of an old woman, gaunt and threatening, advanced towards the bed where she lay awake, her new husband fast asleep beside her. Talon-like hands extended, the woman seized Diane by the throat and squeezed. As the inexorable grip tightened, a horrible gurgling came from Diane's throat. In a mind paralysed by the terror of the unknown and fear of death, she prayed in one lucid corner of her brain that the frantic sounds would awaken her husband, but he slept on, undisturbed. Then suddenly, relief: the fingers relaxed, the arms dropped back as the old woman with a sardonic sneer turned away. Although Diane is not certain that she heard sound she knew that the woman was communicating over and over again, "And now you'll believe in ghosts . . .". Diane screamed. Her husband woke up as the woman hurried towards the door as if to make a normal exit, and then suddenly faded.

The description which Diane Samat furnished of the apparition to her husband, who is Malaysian, was recognised by him as being of his grandmother, a strong-willed woman, now dead, who had brought him up as a boy in Malacca. She was jealous and possessive and had exercised a strong influence over him for the first six years of his life. For days afterwards Diane had a sore throat. The apparition has not returned since that occasion. One other fact worth noting is that the apparition appeared to be lit from within, as if by a candle — the room itself was dark.

When Margaret Collins, an interviewer from BBC radio in Aberdeen, made a recording with Diane Samat about her experience in the self-same room, it was unusable because of an undulating hum in the background. The recorder is independent of mains supply (it is the UHER portable widely used in BBC Radio) and was checked before and after the recording. A repeat performance in the same room proved successful. Regarding this last point, it sometimes happens that the microphone cable of these recorders induces a radio signal on to tape. For example, Blair Armstrong, who does many interviews for BBC Radio Scotland, has twice encountered induction of Radio Two on to interviews done in the vestry of Partick-Newton Place Church in Glasgow. However, Margaret Collins assures me that the hum on this occasion was unlike that kind of interference. Unfortunately, the tape was not retained.

Diana Samat's apparition was paralleled in a number of respects by an incident in 1970 in Fintry, a council housing estate to the north of Dundee. Again it was an old woman appearing to a woman, lying in bed beside her second husband. Again it was recognised as his grandmother at a subsequent date, the woman at the time being unaware of what she looked like. But on this occasion the apparition was benevolent and appeared to be simply looking at the new baby in the pram at the foot of the bed. The husband was sceptical but when the apparition was seen again by the woman's other daughter (who mistook it for her mother at first) he became convinced. The couple are reluctant to have their names published because the husband's family come from "travelling people" (known in Scotland colloquially as "Tinkies") and are superstitious about discussing such matters. Notwithstanding this, as a result of their apparition experience, the couple have begun to attend a spiritualist meeting in Dundee, unknown to the husband's family.

Not far from where the couple now live in Dundee is Morgan Street, which contains tenement flats and a jute mill. It may be said cynically that a ghost is a good ally for a tenant who wants a change of flat. But for two young nurses who were only too glad to get a flat, to run out of it within days with no other place to go, is hardly self-interested. In 1974, Shirley Brown and Gail Bruce (both have now married and have changed their surnames) moved into their new flat. Again it was a case of an old woman bending over one of the girl's beds, apparently talking in menacing whispers. On comparing notes the next day, the girls became frightened. Thus when Shirley heard someone padding about in the kitchen a few days later, she tapped on the wall which divided her bedroom from the kitchen, knowing that if Gail were there she would tap back. But instead of a tap there came a terrible outburst as if someone was trying to batter and claw their way through the brickwork. Shirley called for Gail who dashed in from the bathroom and together they stood horror-struck while the frenzied battering and tearing continued for over a quarter of an hour. They put clothes together to make a hasty exit, then realised that they had left their keys in the living room. As they switched on the light, the bulb fused with a brilliant blue flash. It was the last straw as far as they were concerned and they fled the building and sought refuge with friends. So strong was the reality of their experience that they never again stayed in the flat.

I visited the place in question, now occupied by a family named Hunter. Mr Hunter was intrigued by the story but had not come across any paranormal happenings during his tenancy. He offered the piece of information that the tenement flats are built on the site of the former Mental Asylum which adjoined Morgan Hospital.

In the four incidents recounted above, the percipients were all female. Indeed, Peter Moss found of the four hundred replies he received to his appeal, that the female/male ratio was roughly three to one. Other studies, such as the classic

Gurney/Myers/Podmore work *Phantasms of the Living* and the *Census of Hallucinations*, analysed by Sidgwick et al., have tended to confirm that this faculty of seeing apparitions is much more likely to occur among women than men. A more modern *Census of Apparitions* in 1968 and 1974 carried out by the Institute of Psychophysical Research at Oxford had a total of 1,800 replies of which 72 per cent were women. Surprisingly, the authors of the study (first published in 1975 under the title *Apparitions* and now distributed by the Institute itself) make little of this fact and say that it can only be taken to show the relative frequency in which females/males respond to appeals for apparitional experiences. But as we have noted in passing with regard to poltergeists, it is more than just an idle statistic that fewer men than women have this type of experience. There may indeed be some hormonal tie-up with ability to produce psychic phenomena, but this must remain a speculation, as I am unaware of any research which can confirm or deny it. The only other fact I can cite in its favour is that poltergeist phenomena appear more often in adolescents, who are by virtue of pubescence, going through changes of hormone balance. Research at present seems to be concentrating on a relationship between brain waves and psychic ability, and hopefully this will result in the possibility of a physiological basis being explored. Up to now, the fact of psi has only grudgingly been admitted by the psychologists and been contemptuously ignored by the physical life sciences. Such research might only reveal a *tendency* for certain physiological factors to be linked to psychic ability. For instance, I happened to discover that three of the spiritualist mediums I spoke to were diabetic. That may simply be coincidence or there may be something about the diabetic condition which allows psi-ability to flourish. It may in the end only prove that certain facts about a person's physiology make them prone to hallucinate more often than other people.

As regards the psychological state of those who saw apparitions, I can be more precise in respect of the four cases recounted above. Three of the five women were extroverts, and none was other than sane and normal. The fact is that of the "grandmother" apparitions, neither of the women concerned had seen a picture of the old lady concerned. Thus if their imagination was at work. It was difficult to explain why they

45

were able to supply an identikit picture of their spouse's relative without having known anything about them, unless some paranormal faculty was at work. In any event, in two of the cases the apparition was seen by another person (the Morgan Street ghost and the Fintry ghost).

As for the Red Lion Square ghost in London, Winston Hemmingsley told me that his girlfriend had experienced it and so had a photographic model who stayed at the flat. She was pushed to her knees by a force from behind her while she was in the fatal room. She tried to scream but her face was forced down into the carpet as if "the force" was trying to push her head through the floorboards. She had not been told about the ghost previous to this experience which occurred within a few minutes of unpacking in the room. Thus there is not only corroboration of the stories, but also of the unexpected nature of them. None of the women were full of trepidation that they were about to see a ghost. They were all relaxed at the time — indeed they were lying down. Celia Green and Charles McCreery in their study *Apparitions* asked the percipients to describe their position at the time of their experience and tabulated the result as follows:

Lying down	38%
Sitting	23%
Standing still	19%
Walking	18%

They point out that since most of us spend a third of our lives in a horizontal position, we should not be surprised by the first figure. And they conclude: "On the whole the data do not seem to warrant a conclusion that either increased muscular tension or a state of muscular relaxation facilitate the occurrence of apparitional experiences."

However, in her study on Out-of-Body Experiences (OOBEs), Celia Green found that 70 per cent of these occurred while the subject was lying down and there appears to be a qualitative difference between OOBEs and Apparitions. Occasionally there are instances, however, when a person has had an OOBE and someone else has perceived them as an apparition during their "astral voyage".

During the filming of the television series my most thrilling experience was by no means paranormal. It was a visit to the War Cabinet Rooms beneath Whitehall which form part of a thirty-mile labyrinth of passages, some dating back to the seventeenth century. Just before the last war began, the need for an underground security HQ was recognised and part of this labyrinth was adapted as a Cabinet Room and when Churchill became Commander-in-Chief of the war effort, he moved into his own bedroom adjoining the Operations rooms to keep him touch with the various theatres of war. He made all his broadcasts from a temporary studio in a corner of his bedroom. Another little room contained a "hot-line" telephone to Washington.

The first remarkable thing about this place is that it has been left virtually untouched since the end of the war. (Apparently it was discovered late on in the war that the concrete bomb-proofing would be of little avail against a V-2 missile and so it became discreetly redundant — only when the war finished.) The names of the Chiefs of Staff are still there on the blotters, the scoresheet of enemy planes still chalked up on the wall in the Ops Room. The next remarkable thing is that so few people appear to know about the guided tours which were available until early 1980. Until then the dapper figure of Mr Christiaan Truter, MBE, took round parties of about twenty who had written requesting the tour, which was free, lasted about three hours and was quite the most enthralling museum visit I have ever made.

The final remarkable facet of the War Cabinet Rooms is their ghosts, which are only usually seen by Mr Truter. He has become so used to them that he memorises the names of his tour parties — if he went by numbers he would invariably leave two or three behind in the dark tunnels, their places having been taken by ethereal visitors! The existence of the rooms was top secret and there were a number of entrances through which the scores of personnel who worked there entered. But they could be totally unaware of the existence of others who lived and worked for the entire duration of the war a few feet away behind a brick wall. It is the ghosts of these people who haunt the War Rooms, not as one might expect, the mentally anguished generals or the cyclonic energy of Churchill. They are the humble people whose lives would have been empty without this experience at the eye of the hurricane. Behind them they have left fragments of themselves. Mr Truter, and occasionally one of his guests, pick up the fragments. One is an old cleaner who comes with his brush knocking against the walls. When he comes the lights flicker on and off. A monk from earlier days appears from the knees up, because "in his day the level of the floor would have been different"! The most frequent visitor is a security man with "stone" hands of an odd texture, who is obviously worried by the presence of people in these security areas.

One day, as Mr Truter entered Churchill's bedroom, a hand tried to force his away from the light switch. This came aggressive person then revealed that he had a purpose. He beckoned Mr Truter to a cupboard in the bedroom which had been sealed off. There he found a typed message on the shelf saying, "I have deposited the secret papers of Colonel Hesketh on 4th July 1947 with the LCS", which was then the security unit for that area. Since that message got to its destination Mr Truter has not seen the man again.

When I asked him if he ever saw the ghost of Churchill, he replied: "At first I used to think that cigar smoke in the bedroom was perhaps a sign of Churchill, then I discovered that the ventilation there comes from two floors up, and there happens to be someone on that floor who smokes cigars — so that did away with that. I'm always very careful to check that I'm not just jumping to conclusions."

What then are we to make of Apparitions? Are there any laws or rules which govern the behaviour of ghosts?

As far as modern apparitions go, it would seem that the only rule which governs their behaviour is a "Principle of Unpredictability" — 97 per cent of the Green/McCreery cases were unexpected. (We shall concentrate on this study and leave the classic ghosts to their own haunts of castles and churchyards where legend and atmosphere encourage people to expect them.) However, despite the unpredictability of the apparitions themselves one or two broad principles emerge from a study of a large number of such cases.

(1) *Involvement of Senses*
In the cases discussed the apparition did not always just "appear". The percipients could feel and hear the apparition; hands around throat (Diane Samat); hair across face and conversation (Rosaleen Morrison).

Green and McCleery tabulated their findings of 1,800 cases:

Sight	84%
Hearing	37%
Touch	15%
Temperature	18%
Smell	8%
None of these	4%

They also found that the more complicated types of apparition occurred less often than simple cases.

One sense	61%
Two senses	25%
Three senses	9%
Four or more sense	5%

If the apparition is an hallucination, it is not remarkable to find the senses involved. When dreaming, subjects react to stimuli in the dream as if their sense organs were actually experiencing touch and smell. Under hypnosis, a subject will eat an onion and taste it as an apple if told to. However, the percipients of apparitions are often wide awake and moving about — they are not asleep and are not dreaming in the way that psychological laboratories have learned to detect by the presence of REM (rapid eye movements). Nor are they under the influence of hypnosis or in a state of heightened suggestibility. However, the state of the percipient's mind is not irrelevant.

(2) *Altered States of Consciousness*

There is a definite relation between dreaming and experiences of psi-events. The unconscious mind (which appears to play a large role in ESP) is given more expression in dreams, a fact that is made use of in psychoanalysis. The Maimonides Dream Laboratory has systematically analysed dreams and even had success in establishing that subjects can and do dream about a "target" which is only revealed to them the next day, thus demonstrating an element of precognition at work. Precognitive dreams have long been recognised, cf. Ancient Egypt and the story of Joseph in the Old Testament. Prophets and seers received "a word from the Lord" in the form of these dreams. But even if they interpreted it as divine revelation they were always aware that they had been dreaming when they awoke.

49

There is, however, such a thing as a *lucid dream* in which the subject is aware that he is dreaming at the time of the dream. It is akin to the Christos experience, which we shall look at later in the chapter on Reincarnation. It is also akin to an OOBE. However, one important difference is that the percipient of an apparition does not always realise that he is seeing an apparition until afterwards it is revealed as such. There is no apparent altering of the state of consciousness. Furthermore, lucid dreams and OOBEs can be induced by learning techniques and this does not seem to be the case with apparitions which may only be seen once in a lifetime whereas OOBEs and lucid dreams usually occur several times. Certainly autophany (i.e. seeing an apparition of oneself) may seem the same as an OOBE, the physical body (or soma) is seen from the outside — what Green/McCreery call "autoscopy" — and there is dissociation of consciousness from the physical body. The fact that there is a difference in kind between autophany and autoscopy is reflected in the survey, which had only ten reports of autophany as opposed to over three hundred autoscopy. Autophany is recognised in folk legend by the *doppelganger* whose appearance is said to bode ill. Such a tale is recounted in James Hogg's *Confessions of a Justified Sinner* which is comprehensible as a tale of mental illness and murder or of repressive religion and the supernatural, or a permutation of all four.

The supernatural defies neat categories. Hallucinations of all sorts are possible. Hypnotists can make subjects perceive all the women in a theatre audience without clothes on (I have seen this done by Robert Halpern, who is discussed in the chapter on Psychokinesis). Patients with forms of schizophrenia hear voices and see figures. Delirium Tremens (DTs) sufferers see rats, snakes and pink elephants. Acid-trippers on LSD perceive hallucinations of all sorts because of the drug's effect on their brain. Should we then look for the cause of apparitions with clinical tools? The answer must be no for several reasons. Some apparitions, for instance, are witnessed simultaneously and the chances of two people having the same distortion in their brain chemistry simultaneously can be dismissed. Nor does mental illness occur for the two minutes in a lifetime that an apparition may take up — there would be other signs of hallucination behaviour, which is not the case for the vast majority of apparition percipients. Similarly, drug-induced hallucination can be traced to an intake of narcotic substances which affect consciousness and behaviour in unselective ways that apparitions do not. Finally, it is also the case that hypnosis requires a subject and a hypnotist and an implanted suggestion: even allowing for auto-suggestive hypnosis, it does not explain why Rosaleen Morrison knew the girl's name was Hilary.

In a recent book, *The Paranormal*, Stan Gooch argues that there is no such thing as a ghost. Aside from pathological and toxic states such as the ones I have mentioned, he concedes that hallucinations can occur and when they are accompanied by the acquisition of information by paranormal means (e.g. the name of the girl Hilary) the two together make a "ghost". This appears quite unnecessarily pedantic and it is rendered more absurd by the fact (which he cheerfully ignores) that two people can have the same hallucination and acquire the same information at the same time. Perhaps they exchange the information by telepathy, but he cannot have it both ways — i.e. telepathic hallucination. It is much easier to accept that there is such a thing as a ghost than a telepathic hallucination even if we do not understand its precise relation to the minds who perceive it or the 4-D universe on which it impinges.

(3) *Collective Apparitions*

Admittedly these are rare but the fact that they happen is sufficient to cast doubt on the theory that an apparition is an hallucination of the mind. The girl and her mother in Fintry both saw the husband's mother as an apparition at different times; the apparition of Hilary affected succeeding occupants of the room in Red Lion Square.

A simultaneous sighting of the apparition of an old man called Robert Bowes crossing a lake in a boat is quoted by Sir Ernest Bennett in *Apparitions and Haunted Houses*. Three people who had just visited him on his death-bed saw the same event and it subsequently transpired he had died at the moment of sighting.

In the Gurney/Myers/Podmore volume *Phantasms of the Living II* an incident is recounted in which the Rev. D. W. G.

Gwynne and his wife witnessed a figure extinguish their night-light while they lay in bed and watched. Minute discrepancies between their two accounts have led some to speculate that they both may not have witnessed the same event; that the light may have blown out in a draught and they communicated the figure to one another after the event by telepathy. However, it must be said that the accounts of witnesses to criminal incidents seldom tally completely, so too much store should not be laid by this. But it is worth pondering whether there is a subjective element in perception of the apparition, especially when it appears to have, like the poltergeist, a relation with human consciousness. Yet ghosts can be detected by camera if we are not to dismiss all psychic photography as fraud. And they are often detected by animals before a human picks them up. It would count as a collective apparition if a dog was to bark and act in an excited manner with no outside stimulus prior to the ghost "sighting". At the very least it would demonstrate that what is being "seen" is impinging on the mind from outside rather than within.

At this point it must be acknowledged that some apparitions are seen by one or more percipients but not by others who are present at the moment of perception. Leslie Weatherhead relates the story of an apparition of a dead girl who called a clergyman out to visit her dying father. He engaged in conversation with her all the way to the house, when she disappeared. He had not realised she was an apparition and when he questioned some workmen on the way home, they said they had seen him talking to himself.

The Morgan Street ghost gave rise to frenzied battering noises heard by both girls. Thus not only was it a collective apparition, it caused sound-waves to vibrate through the house, implying a physical element that was not due to hallucination. In this it resembled the poltergeist. Though apparitions do not usually leave physical evidence behind of their presence, there are obvious areas of overlap with poltergeists. Apparitions do not necessarily depend on the "gestalt" of a house to haunt. They can be seen walking in fields and will "invade" the percipient's home territory.

(4) *Content of Apparitions*
We have already met the Metachoric type of apparition in the

52

St Andrews Cathedral story. There are similar instances in which people have seen visions of a battlefield in full swing. Green and McCreery seem to suggest at one point that all apparitions may be metachoric even though the percipient may not suspect it at first. For example, in one case, a percipient saw someone open his bedroom door and look in at him in bed. On trying to push the door shut he found that it had remained shut all the time and it had therefore been an apparition of a door which he saw.

The apparition of objects is common — if we think about it, the clothes on a ghost figure constitute "objects". But as well as the whole environment of metachoric events, there are also instances of objects such as coats, cars and in one case a cheque is classed as an apparition when it disappeared. There are no records, however, of credits appearing in bank accounts by paranormal means.

Occasionally faces or half-figures or parts of the human anatomy such as hands or feet are reported. More common is an apparition of an animal and, not surprisingly, cats and dogs rank high on the list. Ghost dogs are sometimes seen in company with figures. In short, there is a wide range of type and content in apparition experiences.

(5) *The Paranormal Acquisition of Information via Apparitions*

As we have already seen, apparitions can be of living or dead persons. About two-thirds of the apparitions reported to Green and McCreery were of persons or animals known to be dead. Most occurred within a week of death and the frequency fell off as time passed. But some occurred just after the moment of death as in the Robert Bowes case above. There are many documented instances of such cases, but rather than rely on second-hand files, let me refer to one known to me whose percipient is a reliable witness.

The Rev. Ian Renton, a parish minister in Edinburgh, and his wife Ann, had just gone on holiday to Iona, the mystic isle of St Columba off the West Coast of Scotland. When they left they knew that one of the church elders was dying in hospital. That night Ann Renton awoke to see an apparition of the elder dressed in the distinctive faded coat and hat he used to wear, standing at the foot of their bed. She woke her husband who did not see the apparition; it then faded before her eyes. The next day a telegram arrived from the church's Session Clerk requesting Ian Renton to telephone him. The elder in question had died during the previous night.

Is there some clairvoyant faculty at work which enables the dead to traverse sometimes half the globe to appear at someone's bedside at the moment of their death? Many people experience a "feeling" (which must be classed as a kind of clairvoyance) when something ill has befallen a close loved one. But, as in this case, it need not be someone close to whom they "appear". It could be argued that Ann Renton imagined the event because she knew of the elder's impending death, but she did not know him well and he was far from her thoughts at the time. (Note: her husband failed to see the apparition on this occasion, but on one other occasion in his life he had experienced an apparition — also on Iona — thus suggesting that this "second sight" or lack of it is not a permanent faculty which Ann had and Ian did not.)

In atomic physics when an electron drops from an outer to an inner orbit the change in energy potential causes a photon (light-wave) to be released. Could it be that when the "mortal coil" is shed, that some form of psychic energy sends out an apparition? The idea is appealing, but it cannot be tied solely to a moment of death as the following incident, quoted by Green and McCreery, shows:

> A woman whose son and husband had taken the night boat from Littlehampton to the French coast woke up to see her husband in the room. She reached out and touched his coat, enquiring if anything had happened. He replied in solemn tones, "Yes, something has happened." She looked for her son and the apparition vanished. The woman became alarmed that her husband and son had been lost at sea. However, both reached France safely. On comparing experiences later, her husband disclosed that during the voyage when he was unaware of his son's whereabouts on the ship he had had a vivid impression of what it would be like to announce to his wife that their son had been lost overboard.

Strong emotional states and vivid impressions seem to go hand in hand with the creation of phantasms of the living. But if it were simply trauma that gives rise to hauntings of suicide sorts or the reappearance of airmen lost over France, we ought to expect hospitals and funeral parlours to be continually haunted or more people who died violent deaths to figure in apparitions.

As well as spanning distances and flashing back into the past there is evidence that apparitions can even jump into the future.

> I was crossing the River Idle (in Retford) at 10 a.m. I saw a young man sketching and behind him a lady whom I knew, seated on the grass. On reaching them, I saw that he had gone and on enquiring his whereabouts, the lady replied there had been no one there for half an hour. Passing the same spot at 4.30 p.m. I saw the same man sketching. This time he was there in the flesh and I asked him where he had disappeared to in the morning. He assured me he hadn't arrived in Retford until 1.30 p.m.

Was this precognition or telepathy of the artist's intention by the percipient? If it is the latter he must have "transmitted" a picture of himself because the percipient had never seen him before that moment. Note also the absence of crisis or trauma in this experience suggesting there need be neither emotional involvement on the part of percipient or apparition donor, nor need they have ever met.

(6) Recurrent Apparitions

The haunted house in which apparitions or auditory phenomena are detected on several occasions, sometimes with years between, comes under this heading. There are often physical effects such as those which accompany poltergeists (e.g. bangs, knockings or movement of objects) but they are usually of a different degree. "Sightings" occur to different people on separate occasions and there may be some people who act as catalysts to unleash the apparition into its environment. An interesting act of the recurrent apparition is that it appears to yield to suggestion where it is limited to the territory of a house — forms of exorcism and blessing ceremonies often prevent its recurrence. (Some would argue it is not suggestion, but the Holy Spirit exorcising the ghost. However, medicine men appear to have as much luck in achieving this expulsion as do ordained clergy.)

Recurrent apparitions affecting one individual are less

common but they do occur. Green and McCreery tell the story of a woman who saw a stone effigy on several occasions in Tewkesbury Abbey before she realised it was an apparition. Her children also saw the statue in a niche which to everyone's knowledge had always been empty. It would be interesting to find out if the "knight" which she saw had ever occupied the niche during the long history of the Norman church.

Conclusions

Probably the most that can be said is that "some people sometimes see something" which qualifies for the description of an apparition. Whether it exists independently of the minds of those perceiving it is difficult to establish, although animals apparently can detect ghosts. Dr George Owen, the poltergeist authority and geneticist, concocted an intriguing experiment with a group of friends. They "invented" a ghost, named him Philip, and gave him a biography of a Middle Ages nobleman. Through seances they received communications from him and he behaved consistently with his "character", except in one instance. The serving wench whom he jilted to marry was of no consequence to him and he disagreed with his creators that this was morally dubious behaviour, an attitude which would have been consistent with a person living in his epoch but not to a modern. The artefact apparently now had a mind and morality of his own!

That story illustrates how difficult it is to say anything with certainty about apparitions. Statistically, some facets of their behaviour are more likely to be experienced than others. But for every established principle there are contradictions. It is worth noting that when some ghosts' figures have been approached, they appear to have "reactions" which cause them to hurry away as if trying to avoid being caught. Others behave like a mirage and dissolve before the eyes of the percipient.

Science has recently learned how to produce apparitions for itself with the invention of the *hologram*. A 3-D image of an object can be created by reconstructing it with laser beams. It looks totally real to the eye but a hand reaching out to touch it will pass right through. Perhaps some day science will learn to reproduce the hundred and one tricks of ghosts, whose secrets still remain in the minds of their beholders.

Chapter 3

Psychokinesis—Mind Over Matter

The moment when the sauce bottle slid, apparently unaided and untouched by human hand, along the formica kitchen top in Robert Halpern's kitchen, was an exciting one for me. It was the first time I had witnessed such a feat performed and it seemed to break all the rules of science. The beauty of such psychic phenomena is that they bring into sharp focus the question of whether they are genuine or not. The sauce bottle was either moved by paranormal means or by trickery. There is no in-between position. The stage is thus set for the bitter battles which go on in this field between psychics, investigators and sceptics, more of which anon.

But even if metal-bending and object-moving are proved to be a fact, the further question arises as to whether such powers are trivial and useless. If you are given the keys to the Kingdom of Heaven, what earthly use is it to be able to bend them by paranormal means? The answer is two-fold. First, if such powers are established then it may have profound implications for our ideas of known forces. After all, the uses to which electricity and electro-magnetic radiation could be put were not realised when they were discovered a century ago. Second, such mind-over-matter powers may help to explain psychosomatic illnesses and cures and, conversely, they may provide a model for understanding how the non-material "spirit" which many believe to survive bodily death can attach itself to the physical brain during life and exert influence over our bodies.

Psychokinesis is perhaps the most attractive of paranormal powers to the modern mind. Its effects are tangible, measurable, and do not involve the acceptance of any occult theory or religious belief. Here, it might appear, is at last a repeatable experiment physically manifesting psi and making possible its measurement in controlled conditions. But that is just what it is not. Even although spoons have been bent and can be photographed and measured, and this feat repeated by the psychic, there is still not universal acceptance of this puzzling phenomenon among scientists.

The medical term "psychokinesia" is defined as "a fit of violent temporary insanity or maniacal action, due to defective inhibition". But there is little connection between this and the phenomenon known as "psychokinesis" (PK). The medical term is used to describe something about the human body and while there have been observed changes in brain wave patterns during PK, it usually takes place without such twitchings of the body as the medical definition implies. Furthermore, PK is concerned with "action at a distance" — the movement of objects without bodily contact. J. B. Rhine defined it as "the extra motor aspect of psi: a direct (i.e. mental but non-muscular) influence exerted by the subject on an external physical process, condition or object". This does not entirely resolve all the difficulties. What about levitation of the subject's body? In this, the PK would seem to be at work on the earth's gravity force, yet the effect relates to the subject. Or what about the experiments in which rats or cats are "willed" by the subject into performing certain acts? Is this telepathy or PK? For the purposes of discussion, I will assume that PK is an appropriate term for both these cases and go on to list a number of examples and difficulties which they pose for any paraphysical explanation.

Action at a Distance
There are many stories of medieval monks who levitated and even flew, as a by-product of their spiritual powers. The prime example of this is the account of walking on water by Christ in the New Testament. But even if modern PK could be shown to make these events possible, they are clearly an impossible starting-point as evidence. More modern claims of levitation are put forward by the transcendental meditators (TM) of Maharishi Mahesh Yogi at his "University" in Seelisburg, Switzerland. TM practitioners can, for a heavy fee, register for the course in *sidhi* techniques which, it is claimed, will allow

them to levitate while in a state of meditation. Photographs have been taken of cross-legged people bouncing around a room in pogo-stick fashion, a foot off the floor. But the Maharishi's followers will not permit this to be filmed or scrutinised by outsiders, so their claim cannot be counted as good evidence.

Another recent case is that of Padre Pio, the Italian priest who is alleged to have flown — although he was more famous for his "stigmata", bleeding wounds in his hands and feet by which he simulated the crucifixion marks of Christ and which appeared while he was saying Mass. He is now dead and there are moves to promote his canonisation, but during his life the Vatican, partly through embarrassment at the attention he was creating and partly for his own protection, tucked him away in an obscure monastery. Thus the accumulated evidence is not good.

More reliable is the evidence regarding the two great physical mediums of the last hundred years, Daniel D. Home and Eusapia Palladino, catalogued by Brian Inglis in his book *History of the Supernatural*. They both produced levitation and "apports" — objects which were apparently dematerialised and rematerialised elsewhere — as well as movements of physical objects. The evidence is impressive, but it is historical, not current, and science is usually suspicious of non-repeatable experiments. As is the case with the other "religious" PK incidents, if we apply the simplest of all explanations we would conclude that since no one is producing these effects nowadays it is the credibility of the evidence which is to be doubted. Certainly physical mediumship has fallen off since Palladino's day and there are remarkably few PK mediums among the host of post-war clairvoyants.

Between the wars, J. B. Rhine evolved a more controlled way of testing PK and used ordinary people as well as mediums as subjects. They were asked to influence the way in which dice would fall and some impressive results were achieved with a large probability against chance. In the 1960s John Beloff of Edinburgh extended this notion to the random generation of atomic particles by a radioactive element, and subjects were asked to affect the count-rate of a geiger counter. The idea was taken further by Helmy Schmidt, who in the 1970s lashed up randomised radioactive decay of an element to a random number generation (RNG), which was essentially an "electronic coin-tosser". It offered distinct advantages over coins, dice or other mechanical devices for testing PK. An Edinburgh researcher then developed a version in which the subject could "play" the Stock Exchange by trying to drive up the prices of the shares which he held. This had the advantage of retaining the subject's interest as results had often been shown to tail off when boredom set it. But even this machine did not exclude the experimenter offect — the ability of the experimenter to affect the results, not by cheating but by his own force exerted on the apparatus.

John Beloff has often remarked that he seems himself to possess this in a negative degree — a kind of PK damping on his subjects, whereas another researcher in Cambridge seems to have the opposite effect on his subjects and consistently gets positive results. However, these statistical laboratory experiments prove very little. At best they intrigue by their potential. At worst, they are an abstract statistic of no real relevance. "God does not play at dice," said Einstein in another context and it would appear that too many investigators are still hung up on this type of experiment.

Healing as a form of PK

More exciting experiments than the dice/RNG kind have been carried out using PK from the subject on plants and rats/cats, although because they are living things they are less easily measured and controlled, leaving explanations other than PK possible. However, Esteban, a "healer", successfully influenced the growth-rates of enzymes and seeds which were placed in his healing hands. At the time he was unaware of what an enzyme was (yeast is one such substance, which is organic and influences organic chemical reactions without being consumed by the reaction itself). Thus it would appear that even if the healer did not have a purpose or diagnosis in mind as he healed, PK was still operating in promoting growth. These results have the interesting implication that healing is a form of PK. Much of the evidence in favour of "healing" is bound up with psychosomatic effects that make it less clear to identify or measure any PK at work.

A minister friend of mine told me with delight of a

parishioner who had been exhibiting the same symptoms as his ill spouse and who had successfully had his condition diagnosed by the doctor. "It's a new disease," the man proudly boasted, "called the psychosomatics!" The capacity of the mind to acquire symptoms "in sympathy" or in self-pity or self-punishment is well known. The symptoms often are the product of real illness. Real ulcers are caused by real worries and sometimes by imagined ones. This process can be turned round to advantage by the doctor who administers a placebo or "dummy pill" to keep the patient happy. With his mind convinced he is receiving treatment, the patient wipes away the symptoms and is "cured". One step further is to use the patient's mental power to cure the ulcer in the same way as it was caused. Surely this is an example of PK — mind over body.

There is another factor which suggests that healers can exert PK over diseased tissues, arthritic joints and even conditions such as cancer. One such healer is judo expert and former blacksmith, John Cain. Seven days a week his doormat in Birkenhead is worn thin by callers with everything from migraine to multiple sclerosis. This dry-humoured Liverpudlian resembles John Lennon in his early sixties days and has some earthy and often scathing things to say about many so-called healers and psychics.

His own powers centre round an ability to induce a trance state akin to hypnosis in his subjects, but two psychologists who have been put under by Cain say there is a difference between hypnosis and the kind of trance he induces. During trance induction Cain's pulse-rate doubles and that of the patient goes up in sympathy. His many miraculous successes include curing a hole-in-the-heart baby and a brain cancer sufferer with only three months to live. He appears to have at least some effect in 95 per cent of the cases brought to him. I spoke to Joan, a young woman with arterial sclerosis, who after being given a "death sentence" by her doctor had outlasted it by coming to Cain for healing. He had trained her to "crash out" into a coma twice a day, clutching a photograph of him through which his psychic healing power could be channelled. However, she still makes a hundred-mile trip weekly to his public session at Bromborough Civic Centre for additional "treatment".

It is here on a Wednesday night every week that a

spectacular and dramatic event occurs. Forty or so mattresses are laid out on the floor with pillows at the head. Patients sit upright facing the front of the hall. As Cain mounts the platform, the Space Odyssey music flows out of the loudspeakers. He raises his hands and one by one they fall like flies, flopping back on to their pillows in various stages of coma-like trance. Some use this assembly as a meditation session and for others it provides the force which they need to keep moving through life. I spoke to Val, an attractive young girl who had a year previously been unable to walk because of multiple sclerosis. That night she was doing complicated yoga exercises on her mattress.

Certainly there are some cases of spontaneous remission in such conditions — even cancer cases — but it is stretching credibility to suggest that so many of them happen coincidentally as soon as they meet Cain. He is not particularly bothered by theories about what causes his cures. Whatever the trance is, it gets results, and although hypnosis can remove symptoms it cannot cure disease in the way in which Cain appears to do. Although Cain claims psychic powers such as clairvoyance and psychometry, he is something of a maverick in the spiritualist movement and has co-operated with attempts to expose fraudulent mediums. Spiritualists see healing as done by the medium's "guides" who work on the "astral body" of the patient, whereas Cain does not talk nor does he require "faith" in himself or a Divine Power in order to achieve trance in his clients. Whether it is PK from healer to patient, or something else, it is not easy to tell. Indeed the only proven fact is that Cain cures people. The late Harry Edwards was the last person about whom equally extravagant claims were made and John Cain now seems set for fame. A Japanese women's magazine organised a highly successful tour of Japan for him and the book *Heal, My Son!* by Peter Green is being followed by a biography by his friend, journalist Pat Sykes.

As yet, no definitive study of healing has been made which comes to terms with what is happening and, as far as PK goes, we find ourselves being thrown back on the words of the blind man in the Bible who was asked what had happened to him. He replied, "All that I know is that I was blind and now I can see."

Where then does this leave PK? Trapped in the statistics of

lab reports or in the mists of history and therefore unrepeatable? Fortunately not, because there are still types of psychokinetic force which can be observed and studied. As we saw with regard to poltergeists, a definite link with the mental state of a person (usually young) produces RSPK (Recurrent Spontaneous PK). The recurrence of poltergeist effects makes them possible for study, but their "hole-in-the-corner" nature and apparent mischievous intent to defy the investigator makes them unsuitable for measuring the PK effect. Even if healing and poltergeists are laid aside, though, there are still a number of people in modern times who are producing PK effects — sometimes in controlled conditions — and whose powers can apparently approximate to the scientists' cherished aim of repeatability.

The Psychic Super-Stars

When Rhine's experiments were started there was a dearth of physical mediums. In the last decade, however, there has been an upsurge in the number of "psychics" who do not need the darkened seance room of their Victorian predecessors to produce PK effects, nor apparently do they need the hypothesis that it is the spirits of the dead who work through them. To get the results they do not need to go into trance states. The best known is probably Uri Geller, about whom more in a moment. Ingo Swann is another, whom we will meet in the "Remote Viewing" experiments of Targ and Puthoff in the chapter on Reincarnation. These two scientists succeeded at their Stanford laboratory in conducting an experiment in which Swann caused fluctuation in the reading of a magnetometer located underground behind a shield.

In Russia, Nina Kulagina was reported to have been able to "plant" exposure on a photographic film; rotate a compass needle; stop a pendulum; move various objects. She was investigated by four Western authors in 1976 and although much of the widely sold book by Oestrander and Schroeder, *Psychic Discoveries Behind the Iron Curtain*, ought to be taken with a pinch of Siberian salt, there are good grounds for believing that she is genuine. I have seen film of her moving a matchbox by waving her hands near it and similarly causing a compass needle to swirl around.

The question of authenticity is a major stumbling block in

assessing the Superstars. Their very status as "stars" and the multi-media exposure they receive is liable to net them a very large income from their gifts (it is doubtful if this commercial side to PK exists for Madame Kulagina). The latest Super Psychic, the former poltergeist "focus" from Cambridge, Matthew Manning, has the status of a transatlantic pop-star. All this must raise the question — do they have a motive to cheat and falsify evidence? The answer is yes — they have a very large financial reason for doing this. Previously the only charge that could be levelled against most psychics was that they had "created" the phenomena as attention-seeking devices.

Add to this the fact that temperamentally many of the psychic superstars do not take easily to strictly controlled conditions. They are "creative people" and they need to feel "comfortable" before their powers will work. Geller is often reported to have come into a prepared experimental situation like a whirlwind, restless and unsettling. Often his PK phenomena will happen "offstage" and by-pass the controlled conditions, tantalising the experimenters who will have achieved results but not the kind they could say were obtained under rigorous conditions. If no results were obtained then the psychic can always claim that he wasn't "feeling right". If some of the psychics are expert conjurers, they will be able to pull it off most of the time, but when all conditions are finally tightened, they can say that the hostile or "unhelpful" stringency of the atmosphere did not help them to be at their best.

I dislike imputing motives like this, but the world has shown it is prepared to shower fame and fortune on people, like Geller, who might well regard a skilful con-trick as an easy price for their conscience to pay to achieve these glittering prizes. Perhaps that is why the posse of illusionists and conjurers are out to lynch him. They are led by James Randi ("the Amazing Randi") who is active in the Committee for the Scientific Investigation of Claims of the Paranormal, a mostly American organisation which has pursued Geller and casts more than doubt on his authenticity. Randi can replicate most of Geller's feats by trickery and claims that Geller is a fraud. His trenchant but witty book catalogues the occasions when he says Geller has put one over on the scientists. It is not Geller who is the prime object of Randi's wrath but, he says, the scientists who are fool enough to give Geller respectability. Randi has offered a 10,000 dollar reward to anyone who can perform paranormal feats under his strict scrutiny and points to the unclaimed money as evidence that there is no proof of PK.

However, it must be said in fairness to Geller, that he has not yet been caught cheating. Why should he put his head in Randi's noose when there are plenty of scientists around who will give him a reference into the Psychic Hall of Fame? Among these originally was Professor John Taylor of the Mathematics Department at King's College, London, who appeared with Geller in the celebrated Dimbleby "Talk In" programme and later conducted experiments with Geller in which he bent spoons and other pieces of metal. His book *Superminds* is notable for the pictures rather than the text, which propounds a naive theory of electromagnetic forces causing the metal to bend. If these really were electromagnetic forces they could be measured by present-day apparatus and thus would have shown up by now. The proof of this theory appears to have escaped Taylor and he has now retired to a more sceptical stance towards metal-bending and may well regret his foray into print.

Showmen, Charlatans or Shamans?

The Geller phenomenon spawned a number of mini-Gellers — children who were apparently able to bend metal — and they found their way into the lab of Physics Professor John Hasted of Birkbeck College in London. Hasted investigated thirteen such subjects between the ages of six and seventeen. He used a strain-gauge apparatus mounted on pieces of metal which were to be bent. Care was taken to eliminate outside interference (e.g. electromagnetic, acoustic effects) and no subject was allowed to touch the metal.

By putting three strain-gauges on the metal the distribution of the metal-bending PK force could be measured. This, he concluded, is a globule, shaped like an ellipse and constantly changing size, shape and position. The PK effects were small, but for one subject, Stephen North, they almost reached the stage of being "repeatable". Although no subject was allowed to touch the metal, sizeable strips of metal were affected, aluminium proving the most co-operative material. Hasted found that relaxed scrutiny or "inattentive" watching was most productive but insists that the children did not cheat. He also saw the French magician, Jean-Pierre Girard, bend by gentle stroking an aluminium alloy rod 2.5 cm thick, a feat beyond the human strength of any of those present.

When I visited his lab at Birkbeck I saw a tray of contorted cutlery and two video tapes of Stephen North and Julie Knowles respectively. As I watched the boy stroke the foot of a thin metal rod it bent towards him and twisted. The girl stroked a spoon which became plastic in her hands so that the head of the spoon detached quite easily. If the kids were conjuring they are remarkable for this alone, even without metal-bending powers. Professor Hasted also has a selection of glass balls about six inches in diameter which have a half-inch hole in the top. Inside there are dozens of paper clips which have been opened out, popped into the hole and are now "scrunched" up into sculptures like sea anemones. Unfortunately, the kids do not produce the results under direct scrutiny, the reason given being that they get the metal to bend when they are "relaxed".

One boy performs best in the bathroom, so Hasted allowed him to go there for five minutes at a time, photographed his progress step by step as he emerged, and gave him more paper clips when he returned to the bathroom. The result is a fascinating sculpture. A "control" experiment was done with craftsmen skilled at putting ships into bottles and although the craftsmen could emulate the kids for the first dozen or so paper clips, after that they were left behind. Yet it remains that until they can do the trick inside a sealed glass ball, the sceptics will not allow that PK is at work.

With metal-bending as with nothing else, seeing is believing. During the filming of the television series I was lucky enough to see Stephen North actually bend metal under our eyes — and what was more important from the evidential point of view — under the camera's eye.

We had a couple of sessions with Julie Knowles in her Trowbridge home. Julie is a sweet-tempered, charming and shy girl who is partially deaf and lost her mother, to whom she was very close, in the winter of 1979. That last fact had coincided with a drought in her metal-bending and try as she did, nothing materialised in front of the camera. We were not too downcast, since we did not expect to succeed where so many other film crews had failed, using up dozens of rolls of expensive film with little to show at the end except a slight bend in a fork which could have been done by hand and therefore didn't count as proof.

But the session at Professor John Hasted's lab at Birkbeck College was a different story. Stephen North held his hands near the strain gauge while the pens on the chart recorder chugged in a straight line up the paper, signifying that no bending was detected. (Hasted insists that the best results are ones done without touch — the hands are held near the strain gauge, but never touch it.) Then suddenly there was one deflection. Then another. Soon little wiggles were appearing on the chart which has three pens recording simultaneously. The pen on the right is not connected to a strain gauge — so if all three pens deflect, then Stephen's PK power is affecting the electrics of the chart recorder directly and not the metal. If the two pens on the left move, then it is metal-bending PK alone at work. In this session there were signals of both types.

The cameraman for the series was Garry Morrison, a tall carrot-haired man who was very excited by this. His kindly and cheerful manner had appealed to Stephen and it was obvious that the boy was producing better results because of the atmosphere. Garry determined to visit Stephen at home to see if the camera could catch the elusive bending force on film when Stephen was stroking spoons and forks. They used up a couple of rolls of film before anything happened. When it did the camera was switched off. This happened several times. They had a couple of beers: still nothing when the camera was running. Eventually Garry said in exasperation, "Switch it on yourself — I'm off to the car to pack the gear." It was at this moment that a fork became plastic in Stephen's hands and we were able to carry away some rare film of metal-bending — as it happened.

Professor Hasted has had his work criticised by other scientists. The *New Scientist* of 16 February 1978 reported tests of Stephen North and Girard at Grenoble which produced negative results. The story was headed "Fading spoon bender". The most recent attempts to gain scientific credibility for the paranormal appear to have failed. What then are we to make of this work of make-believe and won't-believe which surrounds modern PK research? When Geller descends on a country as he did on the UK in November 1978, he is featured in a newspaper or television programme and immediately people report watches start going, spoons are bent, and so on. One of his trips was to the top of the Blackpool Tower sponsored by the *Daily Mirror*, who received seven hundred letters and two hundred telephone calls following the incident. It was reported that in the tower Geller had turned a compass, bent spoons and restarted irreparable watches, and this was duplicated in homes up and down the country. No mean feat! Randi claims he produced a similar response when he posed as a psychic on an American radio station and accounts for his results by coincidence and suggestibility — enough people reading/watching/listening to produce the required number of coincidences. He argues that most broken watches will run for a few minutes when picked up and held in the hand, the warmth sometimes helping to "unstick" the lubricants.

In Britain the leading arch-sceptic was the late Dr Chris Evans, a psychologist at the National Physical Laboratory in Teddington. He possessed a sealed glass ball with a spoon inside on a glass pillar. The failure of PK subjects and experimenters to take up his offer of this for use in PK experiments confirmed him in his belief that the metal-bending kids were cheating and the investigators were less than rigorous.

Chris Evans was also a member of Randi's CSIP and debated on television with Colin Wilson, the noted and prolific author, on paranormal and occult topics. Both men were excellent communicators, but it was like a jousting tournament in which the knights were thundering up and down different paddocks. Their presuppositions and interpretations of facts/theories never matched. It wasn't so much a draw as a no-contest. This is a problem with PK in particular (and also other areas of paranormal) — what I have called the XYZ syndrome. Until the scientists are agreed upon the facts, it is unlikely that anyone will come up with a satisfactory theory. Some scientists cannot see the wood for the trees or the metal for the girders. Perhaps metal-bending PK will end up in the same limbo as dice-throwing experiments — unable to be fully accepted scientifically and limited by the trivial nature of the effect.

I cannot help having sympathy for the CSIP position when perusing *Uri*, the biography by Geller's mentor, the scientist Andri Puharich, who discloses that Uri's power comes from extra-terrestrial beings in UFOs. That is even worse than Geller's own claim that you can place objects on his photograph and they will be affected. It appears that his inert photograph can perform feats which the flesh and blood Geller cannot always do. Geller has even reported that he has been involved in experiments of a secret nature with the military in the USA. These presumably involved putting psychic powers to uses more potent than bending spoons and mending watches. Ingo Swann has also written a novel entitled *Starfire* which involves a psychic using his powers for espionage and military purposes by penetrating the computers of a rival power.

Far-fetched as both these ideas are, they are put in the shade by a book called *The Philadelphia Experiment* by Charles Berlitz, author of *The Bermuda Triangle*, which was so devastatingly discredited by the "Horizon" television programme a couple of years ago. Mr Berlitz "investigates" the disappearance and reappearance of a US Navy ship and its crew during the war, caused by an invisible ray using hitherto unknown secrets which Albert Einstein had unsuccessfully tried to keep from a world "not ready" for them. Proceeding by unsubstantiated reports, anonymous letters from a crank and inferences out of thin air, Berlitz "finds" that the crew went mad and the Navy mounted an enormous hush-up operation.

Books like this are liable to give PK or any other psychic phenomenon a bad name among intelligent readers and to discredit the genuine researchers. But if another publication is to be believed (why not?) the Russians must have precognition of all this, for in *The New Soviet Psychic Discoveries*, authors Henry Gris and William Dick have assembled "a gigantic jigsaw puzzle of secret Soviet endeavours to conquer the human mind — leading to one hideous and inescapable conclusion: Russia's motives in furthering psychic research are concerned with the domination of her enemies in any future conflict". In the book the authors quote interviews with "the man destined to lead Russia's corps of hypnotists in the next year; the man who is developing a laser death ray against the Chinese; and a man with power to nullify gravity".

Now that really would be beyond Mr Randi — or would it?

Robert Halpern

So far I have sat on the fence in this debate, because I have been dependent on second-hand accounts of superstar psychics. (When I spent a day with Ingo Swann, it was to talk about and not to demonstrate his psychic powers.) However, I have had the opportunity to witness another PK practitioner who has much in common with the Girard-Geller style. He is the Edinburgh-based stage-hypnotist Robert Halpern, who claims paranormal powers in "object moving". He does not use this in his act, which is a highly polished, popular and money-spinning one-man show involving the usual tricks of inducing somnabulistic "volunteers" to perform robot-like at his behest. He often concludes the act on a macabre note by hanging himself — dropping ten inches with a noose around his neck after hypnotising himself to stiffen his neck muscles. From this you may gather that he is a showman *par excellence*. In fact he was brought up as an orphan in North London. He discovered his object-moving PK by accident but has not been slow to realise that it would provide good publicity for his act. Extrovert and talkative, he is in the Geller mould and I do him no unkindness to say that he is not the kind of subject whom scientists would readily suspect of being authentic. Although he does not profit financially from PK, he would do so in a subsidiary sense. He does not like to be put to work like a sheepdog, but he has expressed willingness to have his powers tested by journalists and broadcasters.

Alison Goodall, of the *Sunday Mail*, first met Halpern for tea in the lounge of the Caledonian Hotel in Edinburgh in January 1978. He made a pen on their table roll over. Then, to her astonishment, an ashtray on a table twenty feet away moved along the table. A man at the table shot out his hand to catch it. Next, a teapot at another table occupied by two ladies slid from left to right. Alison Goodall says she can't think how he could have done it. She then took along Astronomy Professor Archie Roy of Glasgow University, an SPR member and experienced parapsychologist, to Halpern's home, where after some failures he moved a milk bottle six inches along a formica top. Professor Roy could not explain how he might have achieved this by trickery. However, Halpern failed to move plasticine

70

inside a sealed jar which Professor Roy had taken along. He explained that he was suffering from influenza at the time, and was not feeling at his best.

Halpern also claims success with turning taps on and off and flushing lavatories by PK! When I called on him, we had a coffee-table session with several objects but, under my rigid gaze, nothing budged. We went through to the kitchen where he moved the milk bottle for Miss Goodall and Professor Roy. I selected a tomato sauce bottle and Halpern put it on the formica top eight feet away and sat beside me. After thirty seconds, it slid towards us about two inches, halted, then moved another six inches. Halpern was jubilant and rushed over to the bottle, followed by me. (I record this in detail, because it must be said that if he was using a loop of micro-thin thread, it could have been looped around the bottle and swiftly removed.) The conditions were therefore not stringent enough to merit a definitive verdict. However, it must be said that in order to move the bottle in this manner without rocking or toppling it, he would have needed to know in advance that I would choose that bottle and construct a loop to pull just at the centre of gravity of the bottle (about two-fifths of the way up). That is what I saw and several other journalists have written stories about Robert Halpern's PK abilities without being able to detect trickery.

Mind Photography

The force with which psychics appear able to influence objects and to bend metal has never been isolated and identified. A certain amount of control over the force appears impossible, but not always. The film of Nina Kulagina huffing and puffing over a compass needle shows that the psi genie is not always easy to conjure out of the bottle. Reports say that Kulagina's pulse-rate can rise to an amazing 240 per minute while she is demonstrating her powers, although it should be added that other "big names" such as Swann, Manning and Geller appear to be able to produce their PK without much sweat. None of these psychics can claim, however, that they have their PK force under their control — there are good days and bad ones. Occasionally the effect is there but it is small, they do not have control of the genie when it comes out of the bottle of their minds.

71

But if this force cannot be controlled or identified, what is it? The answer is that no one can yet be sure. It is not electromagnetic. It appears to have a definite link with the state of mind of the psychic. But is it as meaningless as a puff of breath which moves a feather, or does it carry some intelligent content? That there is a coherent intelligence behind the force is further suggested by a new devlopment made possible by the polaroid camera. It has been called "Thoughtography" and consists of photographs taken pressing the camera against the forehead of the psychic in question, sometimes with the lens cap still in place, and tripping the shutter. Photographs have been produced which show an object or subject which had been the target the psychic was aiming for. Others have only been identified at a later date and appear to have a tenuous connection with the target.

Foremost in the field was Ted Serios, the Chicago bellhop, due largely to the study of his powers published by Dr Jules Eisenbud in 1967. The most remarkable of his productions went straight on to video-tape at KOA-TV in Denver. They first show Serios' face (at which the camera was aimed) — a cloud-like formation over his face then grows larger and develops progressively clearer detail until a completely different picture emerges, clear in some parts and blurred in others. No one could figure out how this might have been done by trickery.

Randi and the CSIP have alleged fraud, but the strength of the evidence furnished by Eisenbud is the use of the Polaroid camera which provides an instant monitor of the result and eliminates tricks in the darkroom or of double exposure. Serios found that by holding a small paper cylinder against the camera lens (he called it his "gismo") he achieved better results. This resulted in suspicions that some trick might be involved but after countless tests conducted under Eisenbud's gaze, the doctor became convinced that Ted used his "gismo" much in the way that a clairvoyant uses a crystal ball to kick their mind into orbit, a focus for concentration. Many of the tests done by Serios produced "whities" — or "blackies"; respectively severely over- or underexposed photographs taken when masking tape had been wound over the lens. Control shots were taken with Ted "not trying" which yielded a normal shade of exposure.

Ted Serios was not the most ideal of subjects for such

72

experiments — he had a recurrent drink problem and by the late 1970s had dropped out of prominence. Not before discovering a protege in Willi Schwanolz, a fellow Chicago citizen. But another contender for the photographic hall of fame is Masuaki Kiyota, who has produced photographs of buildings taken from unusual angles. In 1979, he visited London and was filmed by Granada TV. He produced photographs which looked like a Scots Guard taken by a tourist, but these were only discovered after he had been resting in his hotel room. An amateur magician and intrepid agent for the CSIP, Mike Hutchinson was on hand to point out that hotel bathrooms make ideal darkrooms. He went further and, using a slide of the kind sold to tourists, he rigged up a pin-hole camera with a cardboard box and reproduced a photograph similar to that of Kiyota. The Granada film has never been shown.

Whether or not the credibility of Kiyota was in doubt on that occasion, there is a strong point in favour of some Thoughtographs being genuine. A good number are taken from angles which would only have been possible using a helicopter. (Both Serios and Kiyota have had examples published of multi-storey blocks taken from ten storeys up in mid-air and a hundred feet to the side.) There is also an intriguing element by which details are added to or subtracted from existing buildings or objects, so that the "photograph" is really a mental construct which differs from the real thing in several respects. A surrealist photograph!

Another intriguing feature was demonstrated by Serios when Eisenbud asked him to shoot for "Qeen Elizabeth" as target. Eisenbud had been thinking of the monarch, but the ocean liner of that name came up on the print. This would again point to a relation between the agent or psychic's mind and the content of the photograph. There are lessons here for the poltergeist investigator — what goes into the agent's mind can be transformed and projected back with physical effects. An idea that is "planted" can produce offshoots in other places.

Thoughtography also has implications for Ghost photographs and "Skotography" — the production of "spirit" images on unopened photographic plates. If some mind, once-living or still alive, can produce an apparition which is recognised as a Ghost by some witness, could the same force which produces the Thoughtograph not be at work? In other words if I go to a seance and the medium produces a recognisable photograph of my dead father, then I cannot claim this as conclusive proof of Survival. The medium may have the PK power to imprint photographs on film, using information which I supplied in the form of a mental image. If the human mind can print photographic images, it can, as likely as not, tap other minds for information.

The Electronic Voice Phenomenon (EVP)

The camera cannot lie, as far as British law courts go, and photographic evidence is allowed. This, however, does not extend to the tape-recorder, despite electronic means now available to determine whether a tape has been tampered with or been edited. As a BBC radio producer for some years, I am well aware (like ex-President Nixon) that tapes can be ingeniously edited and "doctored" in order to produce interesting effects. Thus tape-recorded "evidence" of paranormal voices produced by PK from the experimenter or "entity" should possibly be treated with suspicion. However, it is interesting that those working in this field have not been accused of cheating, but rather of being too naive by treating background radio signals as paranormal voices or selecting speech patterns out of random noises as intelligible communications. These voices are the Electronic Voice Phenomena (EVP), now researched worldwide. These may well give a less subjective and more fraud-proof method of receiving paranormal information than the sitting room seance. So what is EVP?

Frederick Jurgenson, a Swedish TV producer, film-maker, writer and philosopher of Russian origin, noticed intrusions on tape — strange, lyrical voices speaking in a mixture of tongues. Jurgenson homed in on these "communications" and himself became the target for clever, precisely beamed transmissions which at times infested any electronic receiving apparatus in his immediate vicinity. A new factor emerged which led eventually to worldwide interest in what became known as EVP. It became clear that concentration by an experimenter on these strange transmissions tended to evoke a positive response from the source of voices, irrespective of whether he was concentrating verbally or mentally. The voice source appeared to be aware of his thought, motives and intentions. This is a difficult pill to swallow, but all successful voice experimenters appear to confirm the fact. Of course EVP has its critics. The perceptive writer on parapsychology, Stan Gooch, in his book *The Paranormal*, dismisses EVP largely on the grounds that tape-recorders pick up stray signals from local taxis or police radios.

Typical of this is the time when an experimenter was having trouble with interference crackles caused, it transpired, by fluorescent lights in the corridor outside. Before this emerged, an EVP voice popped up with the words "It's the Fluoresco". The last word was a "made-up" word or neologism, but the message was clear.

During the sixties, after amassing over five thousand samples, Jurgenson published a book, *Radio Link with the Dead*. He gave several press conferences. At this stage nothing was published in English and only sketchy reports filtered through to British and American magazines and journals. A vital and, to some people, disturbing factor then emerged. Jurgenson could, under certain conditions, speak to and hold dialogue with the voices. He obtained sensible answers. The unknown voice source seemed to read his thoughts, to be aware of his actions, his surroundings, his reading matter. This was the beginning of dialogue.

To distinguish themselves from normal broadcast sources the voices rarely used any language in its pure form. A sentence rapidly enunciated might contain the elements of three languages with the rules of grammar ignored. Strange neologisms were employed. Despite this, in a strange and persistent way the voices always managed to convey a message. The fractured sentences seemed to hang together. Emotion and urgency were conveyed. Compelling female voices informed Jurgenson musically of his mission. "One has the impression that these voices do not know how to speak properly. They sound as if they are stumbling through alien tongues."

In 1965 a Latvian psychologist, Constantine Raudive, visited Jurgenson in Sweden and studied his techniques. Returning to the Black Forest in Germany, he embarked on his own programme of research, bringing to it considerable linguistic skill and a painstaking and stubborn devotion to detailed work, which later seriously affected his health and probably shortened his life. The voices became known as the "Raudive Voices". At this point Jurgenson and Raudive adopted rather varying techniques which were later to become the subject of fierce debate. Jurgenson was talking about spontaneous, often very loud voices intervening on certain broadcasting frequencies. Raudive was seeking to extract faint voices from "white noise", transmitter roar and other amplified sound sources. Jurgenson was satisfied to receive passively what the voice intelligence put across, but Raudive was pushing impatiently ahead and many of his interpretations fall foul of critical analysis. Raudive, who understood several European and Slavonic languages, insisted on placing interpretations even on faint quality voices which could well have been distant broadcasting stations. He even claimed that the fainter the voice the richer the content and this brought the wrath of many parapsychologists down on his head.

Undoubtedly his acquaintance with too many tongues encouraged him to fit interpretations even onto faint passages. At the same time there is no doubt that he did in fact record much paranormal material. The term "Raudive Voices" became adopted in the UK and in the USA and the joint production, the book *Breakthrough*, became the seminal work. But not long after the publication there began distant rumbles of criticism. Some of Raudive's interpretations failed to stand up. One or two were identified as normal transmissions. His fainter voices failed to be verified by common consensus. Raudive, though, refused to budge from any of his interpretations. A young British researcher, David Ellis, together with Manfred Cassirer of the SPR, travelled to Germany to investigate, but returned to the United Kingdom with a strong hint that the "Raudive Voices" were a subjective phenomenon. Ellis proceeded to publish his report, a strong rejection of Raudive's theory. Although these reports dampened down the ardour of British researchers, three others conducted their own experiments and arrived at the conclusion that the voices were in fact objective and paranormal — Richard Sheargold of Maidenhead, veteran SPR member and radio ham; Spencer Wilson of Leigh-on-Sea; and Raymond Cass, a hearing-aid specialist in Hull.

It soon became clear that not every experimenter could produce the voices. Sheargold thinks this is due to PK from the unconscious of the experimenter not being a universal gift. Others say it is because only some people have been selected as a target by "dead" entities of extraterrestrial intelligences. Cass inclines to the latter view. He writes:

> Why did I succeed where so many failed? I do not know all the reasons but I do possess a radio which has allowed the voice transmissions (a Juliette 4-Band receiver tuned to 127mHz on the aircraft band). Unfortunately this is only operative in one location, specifically my office in Hull. I believe that this is a radio reception "hot spot" . . . nearby is a Mass X-ray unit which may permeate the immediate vicinity with emanations helpful to voice reception. Transported to other locations this "suspect" radio systematically failed to exhibit abnormal characteristics or to receive voices. The general noise background in and around my location in Hull is high and there is clearly a lively energy flux. Just how this favours reception of the voices I cannot explain. The same radio receiver transported to my seaside location at Bridlington operates quietly and with a low level of background interference . . . and an absence of voices. Perhaps from the commencement of my experiments in 1972 I was aided by a happy combination of geophysical factors. This does not however account for the long negative periods. I am in the middle of one at the time of writing and it is my acceptance that the prime operative factor is still the existence or absence of a beamed transmission from a hidden source. With the best conditions in the world the EVP will not be received if the transmitting source is silent.
>
> Basically I think that the EVP is not something we do consciously or unconsciously, but that it is something done to us. There is no guarantee that once having been targets for its emanations it will not withdraw and turn its attentions elsewhere.

What then causes these EVP voices? There are several explanations current.

(a) They are dead or *discarnate spirits* communicating in a new way, possibly using the experimenter's PK as a "medium".

(b)   They are some form of *extrinsic intelligence* (perhaps extraterrestrial) trying to get messages across.
(c)   They are autonomous products of the experimenter's psyche, *subconscious creations*, the results of expectation and psychokinetic influence on the tape.
(d)   They are *self-delusion*, auditory patterns of the mind projected on to random noise.

This last explanation is the one favoured by Ellis and put forward by Gooch in *The Paranormal*. There he quotes examples from Raudive's book and compares the voices to the Roscharch ink-blot tests used by psychologists to "read" the patterns which the unconscious mind projects on to a random shape or random noise. The following are all interpretations derived from a fragment Raudive interpreted as "Tja Mambrin".

c'est mon venir/say mumblings/ze alarm things
come on then/de man brings/demand Denis

Raudive had a tendency to say "This is what I hear. What do you hear?" which implanted an interpretation in the listener's mind. In one set of voices analysed by Walter Uphoff of Oregon and others produced by Veilleux in Maine, thirty-four samples were analysed, of which 50 per cent could not be agreed on. There was a fair agreement over 25 per cent and agreement on 25 per cent. The faintness of the voices makes agreed interpretation a problem, as does the polyglot content — is it French or English or German or a mixture?

But self-delusion does not explain away some of the clearer, louder voices of which I have heard a number from Cass's tapes. He handed them over to an offshoot of the NASA Space Project in Europe, a tracking station which can process signals to eliminate interference and background noise, then feed them into a computer which compares them with thousands of radio signals and terrestrial transmissions. Fifty per cent of the samples failed to match up with any known signal pattern. Listening to the "pick of the EVP" it is easy to believe this, for it has a peculiar metallic, sing-song quality.

That does not explain the origin of the EVP, however. Professor Hans Bender, the eminent parapsychologist from Freiburg, is apparently inclined to subconscious origin as an explanation, as is R. K. Sheargold. It is possible to see a connection between this and poltergeist effects. Indeed

Maurice Grosse reports that EVP impinged on one of the cassette tapes he used to monitor the Hodgson girls, although, having heard it, I am unconvinced this was not just a background voice in a busy room. But the poltergeist has much of the features of an extrinsic source of apparent intelligence. Yet the poltergeist is undeniably linked to the psyche of the "focus", as in the explanation which presumes subconscious creations.

If EVP is an extraterrestrial intelligence as in UFO/Flying Saucer literature, then it is strange that it does not declare itself and confines itself to "stealing" subconscious thoughts and "printing" them, and that so many are of a trivial nature. This objection would also apply if it were spirits of the dead which are at work.

Like many psychic phenomena and especially those with PK content, the EVP is sporadic and unpredictable. It does not come to order (with the apparent exception of Jurgenson). Raymond Cass experienced his last voice in spring 1978 and then a curtain of silence came down. But before it did, he had a rather sensational message. In February 1978, shortly after the murder of Helen Rytka by (it was thought) the Yorkshire Ripper, Cass asked his equipment the name of the killer. Within seconds a signal came through which he interpreted as "Roy Duffy". Later during that session he heard the name "Peter Wilkinson" and sent both names to the police anonymously: both were checked and both dismissed.

My other postscript is personal. When my colleague Marjorie Orr told me she had been to see a Glasgow healer, John Hearn, who had, on instructions from the spirit of Thomas Eddison, constructed a circuit for receiving EVPs, my eyebrows took an upward curve of disbelief. But the day after we both returned from a visit to John Cain's home in Birkenhead and had also visited Raymond Cass in Scarborough, I was having dinner in my neighbour's flat. At midnight she put a record on the small portable record player. In the background a clear and distinct signal broke through which sounded like "R4OR2, R4OR2" repeated rapidly several times over. When I turned the volume of the record down to minimum, the voice got louder. It came at minute intervals and lasted a minute. I went back to my own flat to get a cassette recorder and the signal ceased. On returning, the voice

79

chanted "R4OR2, R4OR4, TIFOK, TIFOK,TIFOK" . . . or so I thought. The accent sounded south-east England in origin. I made recordings and the message went on at minute intervals for the next half-hour before ceasing. If I had thought that EVP was something that happened to psychics or cranks I had learned differently.

It would not be the first time that radio transmissions have been "tuned-in" by the amplifier of a record player. I ought also to say that the message had exactly the same intonation each time, as if it were a tape "loop" unlike the one-off nature of Cass's voices. A few days later I discovered that many more of my neighbours were encountering "breakthrough" on radios, television sets, and cassette recorders, and that these coincided with the erection of a new aerial by a radio ham in the next block of flats. A cautionary tale for any investigator of the paranormal that the simplest explanation is in most cases the correct one.

Chapter 4

Out of Body, Out of Mind—Reincarnation

There was no more sceptical candidate for journeying to a life-gone-by than myself as I lay on the hypnotist's couch. Doubly sceptical, for I was not sure that I would yield to hypnosis, far less come up with a previous existence. I was wrong on both counts.

The place was Stanmore in Middlesex and the hypnotist was Leonard Wilder, a dentist, who has written up his success in regressing Peggy Bailey, the wife of his flying instructor. For me the proof of such experiences is that they bear repetition and yield coherent accounts of the past lives which they purport to reach. The first session with Leonard Wilder was mainly concerned with helping me to wander down memory lane with eyes closed. The second session took me back to earliest childhood when I found that I could recall intimate details of the house and garden where I lived with my parents in Dundee. Wilder judged by the vividness of my recall that I was ready for the "great leap backward". To my own intense surprise, as he suggested that I drift back in time, I found that my closed eyelids were fluttering in rapid eye movements (REM) such as are observed in dreaming by sleep researchers. Sucked into a black whirlpool, I was aware and could analyse what was happening — but I was also aware that I was going into trance. "He's got me," I remember saying to myself with some amusement. Asked to choose a time between 1900 and 1500, I seemed to see the figure 1682 with the "8" glowing more than the others. A peaceful, still blackness descended. Where was I? Questions put to me did not prompt, but stimulated me to describe what were definite impressions — yet all this time my ordinary conscious mind was there, a spectator to the whole process.

Gradually I became aware that my body was older and larger. My head was constrained by a helmet. Could I be a Roundhead, the rational self asked? I felt a beard on my chin — surely strange for a Roundhead. Asked to describe my dress, I felt a belt and a skirt of a tunic beneath my waist. On my legs? Yes, there were woollen tights of a russet brown colour with leather leggings wound up. Of course! The realisation hit me. I was not a Roundhead — I was a Viking!

Now the details came quicker. My name is Harkon. I am a chief resting in his tent on the North-east coast of Scotland. The longships lie down in the bay and are propelled by oar and sail, taking about a fortnight to cross from home in Norway halfway up the Western seaboard, using the Shetland and Orkney islands as "stepping stones". Asked about my helmet I replied it was shiny. (No horns — apparently it is only in caricatures of Vikings that these appear.) "Which coast of Norway?" Wilder asked. "My dear man, there is only one coast," I replied disdainfully. I smiled at the apparent haughty bearing of my "other self" who was obviously indulging this ignorant questioner. The "impressions", which were all that these names and details were, had given way to a more definite personality! "Harkon" was similarly unimpressed by questions about plunder and pillage. "We are a peaceful people. We are here to trade," I replied. Still I remained fully conscious, articulating the impressions from within, in English. Asked whether the dark woman I observed in the tent was my wife I became resentful that this servile slut should be so described. "My wife is a lady," I protested and named her as Margareth. Apparently we possessed a son called Markon. The run had now been going for an hour and I was brought back to full consciousness.

What had been going on? Was this really a person from the past or a product of my imagination, clad in details supplied by fragments of memory and given life in a dream-like charade? Perhaps in 1682 I had imagined really 682, a date when Viking ships plied across the North Sea to Easter Ross in Scotland? I really have no idea. I have very little knowledge of Viking dates, names and customs and in order not to prejudice evidence from future regressions I have abstained from mugging up on Viking lore. Nonetheless, I can now state from personal experience that the level of "reality" in these impressions is certainly higher than using imagination and closing your eyes. Every personality, however, has components which can be teased into life under certain conditions. Dreaming gives them a stage and a backdrop. Normally we are not simultaneously awake and dreaming, but perhaps hypnosis provides this link.

I ought to say that despite my "Regression Session" I am not disposed to believe that there is such a thing as Reincarnation. I have never driven through a medieval town and in a flash of *deja vu* remembered a previous life as a serf (or indeed as a nobleman). However, there is puzzling evidence which can be brought forward to show that even if we do not accept that we can pop up in different bodies throughout the march of history, some people have out-of-body experiences (OOBEs) and others experience altered states of consciousness (ASCs) in which they acquire paranormal information about "past lives". Whether this past life is their own or not is still a very complicated question.

First, it should be said that despite a recent interest in Reincarnation, it is not a new subject. The Greeks believed in it, and called it *metempsychosis*. It is a part of the central doctrines of Hinduism and Buddhism, and still widely accepted as a fact in Eastern countries. A principle of Rhythm in the Universe requires the soul to recycle, as the seeds of autumn are reborn in spring. The principle of Karma dictates that this natural cycle is influenced by the kind of life a person leads, introducing an element of moral purpose. While new Western sects such as Theosophists and Scientologists teach Reincarnation, it has until recently been neglected in Western thought, indeed since 553 AD, when it was declared heretical at the Council of Constantinople. There have been arguments advanced that Reincarnation was part of Christian teaching; for example, Jesus was asked "Did this man sin, or his parents, that he was born a cripple?", and elsewhere in the Bible Jesus is accused of being Elijah reincarnated. However, the general opinion of biblical scholars is that these were issues arising out of the presuppositions and superstitions of Jesus' audience, not views approved by him. So Reincarnation has not been a major issue to Western theologians. Only recently have para-psychologists been taking an interest, because of the evidence produced from various case studies and from techniques such as regressive hypnosis and "Christos".

History—by eye-witnesses

There are a number of people around who believe themselves to be reincarnations of historical figures like Hitler or Napoleon. Indeed there are several people who believe themselves to be reincarnations of Napoleon — most of them are in psychiatric hospitals! It is perhaps fair to say that if someone is to be reincarnated from an era dominated by a figure such as Hitler, there will be a kind of "transference" to take on the mantle of the dictator concerned. "What you resist and lose to — you become."

Nonetheless the occurrence of famous reincarnated is rare. One of the best known is the Edinburgh lady, Ada J. Stewart, who has written two autobiographies, the first entitled *The Falcon*, as King James IV of Scotland, and the second about her own life as a dual personality. Joan Grant, the novelist, has used her own experience of a "previous life" as a princess in the Egypt of the Pharoahs to write several books which include a great amount of imaginative detail. This, she claims, she did not gain by research but from pre-knowledge: sometimes she would write in a trance. However, she might have unconsciously acquired information about Egypt and forgotten it (i.e. cryptomania), or else there may be clairvoyance talents at work eliciting details from the unconscious mind, which her creative abilities weave into her novels.

As Gooch points out, the quality of veridical (or true-seeming) evidence offered by most "second time around" people is low and of the sort that could be dreamt up by a lucid or clairvoyant dream. He cites the example of Dr Arthur Guirdham, a retired consultant psychiatrist in the West country, who has written a number of books investigating his preincarnation as a Cathar. (The Cathars were a medieval heretical sect in the Languedoc region of France, who believed in a Gnostic Dualist doctrine similar to Manichees. They were purged in the Albigensian crusade of 1198 and subsequently hounded out of existence.) In my view Guirdham is not a good example of Gooch's explanation: first, he furnishes countless details in his books which can be investigated (and have been by him), sometimes to the point of turgidity for the casual reader; second, the whole subject of Catharism is not as well researched as other aspects of medieval history (largely because they were heretics, all traces of them were expurgated) and the chances of cryptomnesia are very low. Indeed many of the details given in Dr Guirdham's books were subsequently confirmed. For example the robes of Cathar priests were thought to be black. When Guirdham wrote that they were blue, this was regarded as an error until more modern research by scholars of Catharism confirmed it.

Most of Dr Guirdham's information came from a Mrs Smith, who identified him with a Cathar priest, Roger Isarn, and revealed that she and he had been lovers around 1240 AD. Mrs Smith was a psychic and from drawings and information supplied by her, Dr Guirdham undertook a pilgrimage to Languedoc where he found much confirmed. From his own impressions, Dr Guirdham became convinced that he too possessed this psychic faculty.

Readers who find their credulity stretched by the coincidence that these former lovers should meet up and co-exist normally (Dr Guirdham is happily married), will find it difficult to swallow the next two stages in the story, described in the books *We Are One Another* and *The Lake and the Castle*. In the first, a Miss Mills joined up with Dr Guirdham and revealed psychic knowledge of Catharism. Soon they had established that in the West country there was a *group reincarnation* of eight former Cathars of whom they were able to trace seven by name in the period 1242-4, in Languedoc. But following on this unique idea of group reincarnation, information came to Dr Guirdham from discarnate identities. They revealed to him a succession of symbols enabling him to see, in detail, scenes from past lives as far distant as the fourth century AD. It transpired that this same group first assembled in ancient Rome and was also reincarnated in Celtic Christian Cumberland and as French sailors in the Napoleonic era — eight times in all! All the time they espoused their Dualist beliefs (the idea that spirit and matter, good and evil are in opposition) and in *The Lake and the Castle*, Dr Guirdham claims that as Mithraists in Rome and Celtic Christians (pre 664 AD) they held to a belief in reincarnation.

If this is a mass psychosis of eight people it is certainly a well-documented one and does not explain the accuracy of the information obtained. Another explanation advanced is that Guirdham acquired his information by telepathy. But this does not do justice to the wealth of impressions and details about Cathar life.

I remain sceptical about the *group* aspect. Why do they not advance in their ideas if they have so much experience of Lives? For example, in *The Lake and the Castle* a woman reveals that in none of her five lives had she felt sexual passion. She has obviously had a bad deal in the five consecutive bodies she has acquired. I would prefer to think of this whole phenomenon as being *group mediumship* by which people with psychic faculties "tuned in" to the time and place of the events. Since mediumship is through a person, these psychics assume the characters of people living at that time. What makes the Guirdham experience remarkable, though, is that the group chose names which correspond to real characters in the Cathar period, characters who were identified by subsequent research into obscure documents.

Children and Reincarnation

The existence of child prodigies is often taken as *prima facie* evidence of reincarnation. How else, it is argued, could they have acquired such powers of genius, except by being the reincarnation of a person who already possessed them? The late Dr Leslie Weatherhead, one of the most popular Christian preachers and writers, often spoke in support of reincarnation — an unusual stance for a leading Churchman. In the *Christian Agnostic* he tells of a child musician, Danielle Salaman, who was four years old in 1953 and who played piano before she could talk, composed several pieces of music and could play the works of Mozart who was himself a child prodigy. Another example in the same book is Sir William Hamilton, who learnt Hebrew at the age of three and by the age of thirteen knew as many languages as his years including Sanskrit, Arabic and Malay. At eighteen he was the finest mathematician of his day. But *self-conscious reincarnation* does not appear to have occurred in either of these cases of early genius. Nor did Mozart believe, for instance, that he was the reincarnation of a previous composer. It is unnecessary to explain child prodigies in terms of reincarnation — why add to one phenomenon which induces awe and wonder and one which is *fact*, another phenomenon which involves greater credulity and is *theory*?

However, there are instances of child reincarnation which are *self-aware*. Professor Ian Stevenson of Virginia, USA, is the leading authority on the subject and has collected material round the world, some of which has been published as *Twenty Cases Suggestive of Reincarnation*. A large number of these children had "died" a violent death in their previous life, perhaps suggesting a motive for the persistence of memory. Stevenson checked whether the locations relevant to the previous life could have been known to the children, perhaps while travelling as a baby. Some of the stories were inexplicable by ordinary means or cryptomnesia. There also emerged a suggestion of intent — that the person could choose when and where to be born. Maria de Oliveiro, a Brazilian girl of twenty-eight, died after promising her friend Ida Lorenz that she would be reborn as her daughter. Ten months later, Ida gave birth to a girl who, at the age of two-and-a-half, began to give detailed knowledge of Maria's life to the tune of 120 separate recorded instances.

Leslie Weatherhead quotes the "Problems of Rebirth" by Ralph Shirley in which an instance of a child dying and being reborn to its own parents occurs. Captain and Signora Battista lived in Rome. Their daughter Blanche had a French-speaking nanny who taught her a distinctive cradle song which the little girl loved to sing. The girl died and the nanny moved abroad. Three years later, during pregnancy, Signora Battista had a dream in which Blanche intimated her intention to return. Not wishing to upset his wife, Captain Battista agreed to the new baby being called Blanche. She was never taught, nor had she heard the cradle song being sung but, at the age of six, she started to sing it clearly. When her parents asked her in astonishment how she had come by it, she replied "I knew it in my head."

Colin Wilson in *The Occult*, after reviewing some of Ian Stevenson's cases, declares himself convinced that:

> (a) reincarnation occurs all the time but memory of previous existence is rare; it happens most frequently when the death was violent; (b) 'spirits' seem to have a certain amount of choice about reincarnation; (c) cases in which there is memory of a previous existence occur most often among people who already accept the idea of reincarnation; (d) more than one spirit may occupy the same body.

Regarding these last two conclusions it is worth adding that many of Stevenson's cases occur on the Indian subcontinent where reincarnation is an accepted fact. In these countries it is considered unlucky to be aware of a past life and there is no money to be made from it (always a factor worth establishing in assessing motive for paranormal events).

As for the idea of different persons sharing a body, it should be said that this is not the same as "possession", which is alleged to be by a demon and creates symptoms of psychiatric disorder. Cases of "multiple personality" may result in abnormal behaviour, but not the other distressing effects of alleged possession. Famous examples include the fairly recent "Eve" case about the three personalities of an American woman, and the Sally Beauchamp case studied in the 1890s by Dr Morton Prince. In the latter instance Christine Beauchamp was "taken over" by a personality called Sally who was as extrovert as she was introvert, and who caused endless complications in her life by "living it up". Christine would awake to confront the consequences. Eventually a third personality emerged, that of a prim lady. By hypnosis Dr Prince got rid of the prim lady, but only with difficulty did Sally give up her right to live vicariously in Christine's body. In the other case, Eve's husband had to learn to live with his three wives; but, as Eve disclosed in a radio interview, there are problems if she drives to the supermarket to shop and is stuck there because she is taken over by another personality which cannot drive! These cases have been closely examined by physicians who cannot explain them in terms of known mental illness. For all purposes, the two women were normal. But these cases need not provide proof of reincarnation. They may resemble mediumship in which daytime trance allows the "controls" to enjoy a pseudo-personality.

A man who is not taken over by his other life but who has been conscious and aware of it since childhood is Edward Ryall, whose *Second Time Around* catalogues his existence as John Fletcher, a seventeenth-century Somerset farmer killed at the Battle of Sedgemoor during the Monmouth Rebellion. Ryall has lived all his life in Essex but became aware at an early age that he used archaic words such as "reen" (a drainage ditch, but in Essex understood to mean a dyke). Ryall has been investigated by Stevenson, who has eliminated history books or novels as a source of Ryall's information about seventeenth-century England. He declares that Ryall does not have the intellectual ability to have researched his background so thoroughly as to fool everyone by non-paranormal methods, in other words, by fraud. Nor could he have easily obtained the names of former rectors of the parish or the location of windmills which have long since disappeared.

But in Stevenson's other cases of child reincarnation it is significant that memories of the "previous life" wane as the child ages. Unlike mediumship, which seems to increase in capability with practice, it falls off. To recall "past lives" in adult life other techniques can be employed and it is surprising how many people have produced results through these different techniques.

Regressive Hypnosis

There are a number of psychiatrists like Denis Kelsey and dentists like Leonard Wilder who have practised regressive hypnosis with the object of obtaining reincarnation data. But perhaps the best known hypnotist to use this technique has been Arnall Bloxham, the Cardiff hypnotherapist who for over twenty years tape-recorded over four hundred cases of patients recalling previous lives. The recall became sharper as the sessions were repeated and in 1976 the pick of these "Bloxham tapes" were used as the basis of a television programme presented by Magnus Magnusson. It was produced by Jeffrey Iverson, who has written up the results in *More Lives Than One*. The most interesting of these tapes were: Welsh housewife Jane Evans who recalled *seven* lives, one as a twelfth-century Jewess in York; an unassuming Swansea man, Graham Huxtable, who became a rough-diamond gunner's mate in Nelson's navy; and press photographer John Pike who remembered witnessing the execution of King Charles I. Historical research on these tapes yielded interesting results. An apparent mistake by Jane Evans in describing a crypt to a house in York was vindicated by the excavation of just such a crypt during the filming of the programmes! Naval historians at Greenwich were astounded to discover in Huxtable's tape archaic naval slang which he could not possibly have researched without difficulty. The most dramatic feature of this tape is the re-living of the moment when Huxtable, as a gunner's mate on the *Aggie*, has his leg blown off. Iverson concludes:

> My own view is that the rationalists are not entitled to any walk-over. The Bloxham tapes have been researched and there is no evidence they are fantasies. In our present state of knowledge about them, they appear to convey exactly what they claim; a genuine knowledge and experience of the past.

However, Iverson's strict alternatives between "fantasising" and "literal truth", seem to me too simple. He ignores the fact that ninety-five per cent of the four hundred people regressed by Bloxham offered no special information or veridical evidence. Surely we could expect a little more if the subject is a "character" whose whole life experience is carried with him or her, rather than a lucid dreamer vividly describing personal experience or, as is more probable in these minority of instances quoted above, someone in a state of trance induced by the hypnosis, in which ESP seems to appear more readily.

Arnall Bloxham is now too old to continue to produce new cases. But a Liverpool hypnotherapist, Joseph Keeton, has 150 hours of tape made during regression sessions with a thousand subjects. One Blackpool housewife, Edna Greenan, claims under hypnosis to be Nell Gwyn. Mr Keaton, who does not accept money for these sessions because it would "force results", is the subject of a book *Encounters With the Past* prepared by Peter Moss. Apparently "Nell Gwyn" can remember plays by Dryden in which she acted and although she cannot remember many of the lines, there are several details which are not book-orientated. Frustratingly there are also mistakes in her account and these make it less easy to pinpoint what is happening.

Another most interesting case to me is that of Sue Atkins, a lexicographer, who becomes both Charlie, a cheeky urchin, and Father Anthony Bennett, a seventeenth-century Jesuit priest, who is burned and goes out of life with a shattering thirty-second scream. I tried to trick Mrs Atkins (as Father Bennett) by asking her who her bishop was (there are none in the Jesuit order). She passed the test, but is married to a former Anglican priest and could have known the answer. Again it is frustrating that much of the evidence could have

90

been picked up by her unconscious. Most people are astonished at the wealth of detail retained by their unconscious memory and capable of release under hypnosis. For instance, I might glance in a shop window and see a book and vaguely remember the title. Under hypnosis I could give a detailed description of what was on the cover and even name the other books in the window. This "cryptomnesia" must be eliminated as an explanation before a past life is proved. Unfortunately it cannot be ruled out in a further example.

Frances Isaacsen, an American craft teacher, was regressed by Keeton to the early nineteenth century and answered in Swedish. A Swedish-speaking lady in the room at the time conducted a conversation with her. Unfortunately, it did not extend much further than the kind of thing in Chapter Two of a *Teach Yourself* Swedish book and Ms Isaacsen admitted that as a child she might have heard her grandmother speak in Swedish.

Not so, however, the case of "Jensen Jacoby", the past life of a Philadelphian doctor's wife, investigated by Stevenson in *Xanoglossy*, who was able to converse fluently in an archaic form of Swedish of which she had no knowledge whatsoever. This lady manifested "Responsive Xenoglossy", in other words she could conduct conversations in the alien tongue, not just use the odd word or repeat intelligently remarks made to her. She did have Swedish antecedents and this might suggest there is something to the idea of a "racial memory". This would accord with the fact that so many of the "reincarnated" are born into the history of their own country. Unfortunately, cases like the Jacoby one are rare and most of the "lives" are of mundane citizens, scant in detailed information, which could not have been supplied by the imagination.

The fact remains that even if telepathy or cryptomnesia is brought in to explain the "past lives" of these hypnotic subjects, it is still a remarkable phenomenon. I am equally certain it has dangers if the hypnotist does not ensure that the experience does not stir up extreme emotional states or becomes needed as a regular fix, much in the way that the Chinese sought the dream world of the opium den. There is much in the unconscious mind by way of dreams, symbols, shadows and archetypes. Normally we dream it away during sleep. But if the hypnotist's couch provides a means for the subject to be awake while he dreams, the danger is that those things which properly belong to the world of myth and fantasy will take on the aspect of facts. One could foresee the widespread fascination of the Ouija board, and the fascination similarly aroused in some subjects by the Xanadu world of regression.

Peter Moss likens the possibility of one of today's hypnotic subjects really being a historical figure (like Nell Gwyn) to winning a lottery by buying a single ticket, at the first attempt. He is therefore reluctant, despite the hours of tapes he has listened to, to accept reincarnation as proven. Moss thinks that regression may be linked with ghost phenomena, in that it may be a form of *wish projection*. His survey of ghosts produced a preponderance from urban areas (as one might expect from population distribution) but the number of reincarnation claims from these areas was small (£300 worth of advertisements placed in London and Birmingham only produced six replies). Perhaps there is something about the influence of the social environment which allows self-aware reincarnation to flourish in rural areas as in Eastern or primitive societies. Whatever it is, it would appear that, in Western subjects, devices like hypnosis, producing altered states of consciousness are necessary to bring back the experience of past lives.

Another procedure which does not rely on hypnosis is practised by the Church of Scientology and is known as *dianetic auditing*. This jargonistic phrase is typical of Scientology teaching, which is full of neologisms coined by its founder and guru, L. Ron Hubbard. Scientology is a gnostic-style religion which offers "salvation" by gnosis or knowledge of the elaborate techniques of dianetics — or rather, not-so-elaborate techniques covered with elaborate jargon phrases. The Church of Scientology apes orthodox denominations with pseudo-religious ceremonies whose liturgy consists of phrases which remind me of a style akin to Groucho Marx chewing a cigar and impersonating the Pope. For some reason which they will not reveal, the FBI and the British Home Office consider this sect a danger to mankind.

The Scientologists exhibit zealous charm in marketing their bubble-bath Salvation and were most helpful in supplying material for the study of their teaching and techniques of reincarnation. These were first formulated in 1950 in "Dianetics" — which is defined as "from Greek dia (through) and noos (soul) thus 'through the soul', a system for the analysis, control and development of human thought which also provides techniques for increased ability, rationality and freedom from the discovered single source of aberrations and psychosomatic ills." Quite a claim, even allowing for the mistranslation of *noos*, which really means *mind*. But another book, *Have You Lived Before This Life?*, goes further. It is described as "A complete run-down on the mechanics of *death* — Discover *what death is*, how it works, what happens to people when they die, and why people forget." The book itself is quite forgettable, and catalogues transcripts of "auditing sessions" in which subjects recall past lives. Most of them lack any verifiable content and are of the essence of lucid dreams, for example, one in which someone finds himself living a past life on Mars. Many of them parallel the Bloxham cases in that they end in violent death.

The techniques consist of an auditor (or counsellor) assisting a "Preclear" or PC (someone trying to achieve spiritual progress to the state when they will be *clear*) to recall past incidents which have given rise to psychological or psychosomatic "blocks". This is aided by the use of an E-meter (a galvanometer which measures voltage, used in the way a lie-detector is used to measure changes in electrical potential, for instance, slight sweating will cause the meter to deflect — if fear of some experience is present). The auditor tells the PC to "Move to the beginning of the incident", while he or she is in a relaxed pose and frame of mind. It should be said that the Scientologists do not accept this explanation but talk of "mental mass" being removed (weight off the mind!) so that the needle attains a free-fall position. They even claim that a pre-clear, weighed before and after auditing, should show a weight loss! Since squeezing the fist can produce fluctuation (as might accidentally occur in recalling a tense experience) the whole process is a joke, scientifically speaking. But, as with the Biofeedback ESR machines, in which a voltmeter monitors relaxation by using the electrical skin resistance (ESR) of the palm, the most that can be said is that emotional changes in the subject can register as needle fluctuations.

Ron Hubbard recalled being a Carthaginian sea captain in

the Mediterranean and even went on a voyage of rediscovery which is catalogued in *Mission Into Time*. The pictures are pretty but even if it convinced Mr Hubbard, there is little in the text which would persuade a sceptic that he did not fit the "maps" he drew before setting out to the ambiguous shapes of the myriad islands and ancient ruins which exist round the Mediterranean. Why then have I bothered to give space to "auditing past lives" — which seems a fancy name for the kind of thing psychoanalysis does in helping people to get over mental blocks? The reason is that a Glaswegian part-time taxi driver in his late twenties, who sells alarm systems, came up with some interesting evidence during auditing.

Norman Stewart spent many holidays with his parents near Strathaven in Ayrshire. He felt particularly drawn to go there with friends for outings. He became a Scientologist and during auditing came up with a past life in Strathaven between 1662 and 1722. He was sceptical but enlisted friends, Roddy Mungo and Jim Tweedie, to help him locate a dozen "targets", some of which he sketched in advance. They were: a bridge, a pair of castles, a pair of old mills, a prison, a priory, a church, a gun-fort and burial chambers.

The trio took several trips and photographed each of the targets as Norman Stewart located them by a mixture of intuition, luck and possibly clairvoyance or memory. The priory had been used as a kind of barracks, he remembers, yet his functions had some relation to ecclesiastical life. He also recalled a figure known as St Marr, dressed in a dark cloak, with white cravat and cuffs, wearing leather boots and a studded belt. St Marr came to "baptise" the locals in a deep pool of the River Avon. (At the period he describes the Covenanters were strong in that part of the world and their militant stand against Episcopacy caused them to be associated with insurrections, hence possibly the army and anti-clerical figure.) They once found a church but Norman sensed it was the wrong one. He led them further on to a clump of trees which was hiding the ruin of the church he was looking for. The "Priory" is known by the locals as the "Borlands" and they believe it was built as a market garden for protected fruits. But Norman Stewart disagrees and, to prove his claim, he pointed out the exits of escape tunnels whose swing doors of stone were hidden from view three hundred yards away. The gun-fort had been turned into a rubbish dump — for all the world it looked like the underside of a bridge. But on digging out the rubbish they found the chains used to hold the guns in place.

For Norman, though, the *piece de resistance* which provided him with his "proof" was the discovery of the burial chambers. He drew a map which identified a wooden bridge across the Holeburn at a break in the trees. Both these facets had not survived to the present day. He knew that these burial chambers were used for some religious purpose although they were ancient. They were located near a place "where we used to go mining", yet after six unsuccessful trips they could not locate the spot. The seventh time they waded up the Holeburn from its junction with the Avon and encountered some blocks of stone which they lifted. There was nothing, but Norman had a "feeling" that they were close to something. Twenty yards away there were more stones and he felt sure that this was it.

They began to dig and after four days' hard work had a remarkable find. After uncovering a dummy entrance they gained access to a hidden and previously unknown sequence of chambers which stretched a hundred yards. Whatever it is they found it is certainly of some interest archaeologically: Anna Ritchie, an expert who was shown the photographs, ruled out a burial chamber but was sure that this cleft in the rock had a man-made element in it and might have been used to store arms or supplies or treasure. She dug there herself and confirmed that Norman Stewart could not have stumbled on it by accident.

Norman Stewart feels the find has provided proof of his past life. For that reason he and his friends covered up the entrance and have not yet notified any authorities of the find. No one will find it by accident, he claims, and it is the trump card up his sleeve. I have visited the site and Norman Stewart has shown me the burial chamber. It is well away from the path and could not be stumbled on. This applies less to his other targets, which have been dated as the remains of a nineteenth-century mansion, Muirburn House, which stood on the spot. It was sold for use as a sanatorium but World War I intervened and it stood empty until used by the Air Ministry to test TNT explosives in 1941. A local legend says that the Alston family who built Muirburn earned their riches in the Far East from opium trade and that there was a curse on them and their house. However, it is a Victorian curse not a Covenanter one!

As to the stone doors to the tunnels, these were thought by an archaeologist to be stone slabs used by farmers for standing cattle in. This illustrates yet again how genuine and unusual finds in "past lives" can be mixed up with sincere errors. Yet even if he had "dreamt up" the experience from his childhood holidays, this could not be said for the burial chamber, which had never been excavated before and which corresponded astonishingly to his drawings. However, it does not necessarily "prove" his previous life. He gave a lot of information about buildings and geography which could be verified, but not much detail about people, which might have seemed more likely had there been a "personality" reincarnated in Norman's body. What I am suggesting is that he may have exercised some sort of clairvoyant mediumship akin to water-divining. His previous empathy for this area would have made it easier for him. This theory will become clearer when we look at the next technique.

Remote Viewing

This is the description given to a type of experiment developed at the Stanford Research Institute in California by Targ and Puthoff whose experiments with Uri Geller were mentioned earlier. They have done most of their work with an American psychic, Ingo Swann, who left his job at the United Nations to paint, write and pursue propensities for ESP which became evident in his late thirties. Due mainly to his work with Targ and Puthoff, written up in *Mindreach*, Ingo Swann is now known as a "super-psychic".

He has written an autobiography *To Kiss Earth Goodbye* and a recent sci-fi thriller *Starfire* which tells how a superpsychic wreaks havoc in the world balance-of-power situation by his ability to read secret files and "psych-out" military installations — what I suppose will be called "psi-fi"! Ingo Swann showed that he was capable of describing places anywhere on the globe, given only the co-ordinates of latitude and longitude. Targ and Puthoff named the experiments "scanate" and they produced some remarkable results. That these results could have arisen by chance is out of the question. That they arose by "eidetic memory", in other words, that Ingo Swann had memorised the atlas, is fairly unlikely. That they arose by collusion with the experimenters can be ruled out — a scientist phoned Targ and Puthoff and asked Swann to do an immediate check on 49 20'S. 70 14'E which was Kenguelen Island in the Indian Ocean, a centre for Franco-Soviet weather studies. Not only did he pick out various details (radar antenna, orange buildings) but his map showed a remarkable correspondence to reality.

To further test this faculty and rule out eidetic memory of the atlas, Targ and Puthoff persuaded Ingo Swann to sit in a room while one of them went to a location some miles distant (chosen at random from a number of alternatives, put in sealed envelopes to avoid prior influence of the subject). Ingo then described and drew what they were viewing at a given time. The experimenter took photographs and compared the two. The result showed remarkable coincidence. What is more they repeated the experiment with other subjects, both psychics and those with no proven psi-ability. Although the psychics did significantly better there were surprisingly good results from others. Indeed Ingo Swann makes the modest claim anyone can acquire this ability!

Repeatability has always dogged ESP experiments and until someone else has replicated results it is perhaps unwise to accept them uncritically (as the Cleve Backster results with a lie-detector on plants show). One of the difficulties occurs in ranking "hits" and "misses' in Remote Viewing. Obviously it is more subjective than the mathematical exactness of guessing which of five symbols on a pack of Zener cards will turn up or which of the six sides of a dice or numbers on a random number generator will show. But it has two advantages because of the "uncontrollability". The first is that there is not a one-in-five chance of corresponding to one of five card symbols — it is the much wider field of possibilities which the geography of the earth offers. Thus achieving an accurate correspondence is a much more remarkable event. The ESP faculty appears to work better when the imagination is stimulated and when the body is not. Sensory deprivation techniques known as "Ganzfeld" (pink goggles on the eyes, while lying in a darkened room with white noise in the ears) have produced some interesting results in transmitting pictures to target subjects in the Experimental Psychology

Laboratory at Cambridge. Asked to choose the target picture out of four possibles, subjects working with Carl Sargent have scored up to a fifty per cent success rate. For the second fact about Remote Viewing is that the subjects seem to have much more stimulation and thus are less bored and more successful when the target is not a number or a symbol, but a three-dimensional location.

There may be some who would say it is absurd to suggest that the figures of latitude and longitude can be viewed. These numbers are arbitrary lines drawn on the atlas because of human conventions — why should they tell the psychic anything? Ingo Swann's answer is that they are simply a convenient focus for the clairvoyance faculty. If the psychic used a Chinese system of map references he is as likely to get the same result. He also told me that he tried painting pictures of planets in the solar system by "Remote Viewing". To date, these have not corresponded to anything found by space probes — his picture of Mars and the Mariner probe, for example. However, he added, "I might have gone in the wrong direction and viewed the wrong planet!"

More interesting is the experiment Swann intends to do in archaeology by using his psychic powers. He intends to select events, places and dates and try to pinpoint locations. "We are only interested in archaeological sites which can be checked out properly," he added. "Clearly there would be a lot of money to be made in hunting treasure, if it worked. But we're interested in serious research." I shall wait with interest to see the results. The "Scanate" experiments seem to use map references in much the same way as a psychometrist uses an object such as a watch to focus on and "sense impressions about its owner". In the case of stones and dates from the past being used as a focus for psychic archaeology, the proof of the pudding will be in the digging.

The Australian writer G. M. Glaskin has recently brought this technique into prominence in two books, *Windows of the Mind* and *Worlds Within*. With the help of Christos, a subject can "travel" to other places, identities and times. Glaskin stumbled on this technique in a magazine. Because it is very simple, and because of the high rate of subjects who are able to be "induced", it will probably catch on as a popular way of inducing altered states of consciousness without the travail of

98

prayer and fasting required by mysticism, or the exercises and practice required by Transcendental Meditation. It is also more accessible than hypnosis and is much less difficult to master in achieving OOBEs consciously. Furthermore, the subject is conscious of his immediate surroundings as well as his ASC throughout the experience. However, as Glaskin compounds it, Christos is not simply an ASC, it reaches *past lives*. The technique should not be attempted after drinking alcohol as this can lead to a "bad trip" — and it is probably better to read Glaskin's full description of the procedure which, briefly, is as follows:

(1) The subject lies on the floor with a cushion supporting his head, eyes closed and shoes off. His ankles are rubbed vigorously for five minutes while someone massages the "middle eye" of his forehead with the edge of a hand until a buzzing effect is felt in the head.

(2) The "control" then has the subject "look" (still with eyes shut) at his feet. For twenty minutes he is put through stretching exercises, imagining himself stretched and contracted at feet and head.

(3) The "control" tells the subject (who is now in a highly suggestible state) that he can float up into the air and has him describe the front door of the house. He floats him up to "cloud level" and down slowly. When he touches ground he is asked to look at his feet, describe what he is wearing, his surroundings etc. To end the run, (3) is reversed.

Sometimes Glaskin's subjects, in answer to the last series of questions, described their feet as black or answered that they were wearing sandals. He did several "runs" with friends and got a wide variety of "lives" — his own being that of the leader of an Egyptian community 3,000 years ago. But although he deserves the credit for disseminating this interesting technique, I found both of his books frustrating. The veridical value of the information brought back is small, rather like the "dianetics" subjects. he does not say whether he attempted to take subjects several times to the same life to enlarge on details — and appears to be quite content with one run per person.

Regressive hypnotists require many sessions before they get their best results. If Christos fails to produce the same past life twice running, no doubt it will be argued that there are two different past lives which have surfaced. This would confirm my suspicion that Christos is a procedure for inducing a hypnotic trance state of lucid dreaming rather like the practice of the Regression Hypnotist. Further confirmation comes in *Windows of the Mind* when one of Glaskin's friends, who was a homosexual, found himself being stimulated by a young boy in a Roman brothel. It is perhaps too coincidental that he would have the same proclivity in both lives. To say that Christos subjects are experiencing "lucid dreams" is not to deny the reality of their experience or to exclude the possibility that they may acquire paranormal information during the "run". The results of experiments done by Alistair McIntosh, a science graduate of Aberdeen University, have confirmed me in this view.

Christos Transcended

In his paper *The Christos Phenomenon*, a study of some induced ASCs, Alistair McIntosh recounts the results of experiments done with students (mostly female) at Aberdeen between 1974 and 1976. This paper contains interesting new material on Christos. McIntosh began with Glaskin's book and after several runs came to see the technique as a vehicle to travel what Freud called "the royal road to the unconscious". He was referring to dreams — but in the "lucid dream", McIntosh concludes that we have something that is devoid of controversial symbols, and that by the dual-consciousness of the subject it is possible for the analyst to ask questions about points which might otherwise have remained vague. Thus Christos can be useful in psychotherapy.

But in her study of OOBEs, Celia Green points out that it is sometimes impossible to prevent lucid dreams spilling over into OOBEs. This altered state of consciousness, where the subject seems to observe himself and his own physical organism from outside, is referred to as a *discrete* ASC (d-ASC). McIntosh decided to try to cross the borderline between ASC and d-ASC into OOBEs. His criteria for determining whether a subject had had an OOBE and not a lucid dream was: that the subject should be an objective observer of some event and not a participant — as in the case of normal dreaming; and that the environment perceived should exist contemporaneously with the experience. He "floated" his subjects out into the room and, as they lay with

100

eyes closed on a couch, he would hold objects beneath the couch and ask them to identify them. (Interestingly this experiment was done by French hypnotists working in Mesmerism last century.) This met with some success but there appeared to be difficulty on the part of the subjects in identifying objects — a mug was described as a cup; a pack of cards was described as "something small . . . white . . . a piece of paper?". These efforts were accompanied by rapid eye movements (REM) such as occur during dreaming. One of the best subjects, named Ann, "travelled" to an exam room and correctly identified her friend Paula there as well as the first word of the exam paper. That evening Paula was in her room on the floor above while Ann was in a Christos-induced d-ASC. McIntosh suggested Ann should try to locate Paula:

"Ah," she said, "Paula's sitting in her room on the hard-backed chair [actually she was sitting on the bed] and she's talking to a girl I've never seen before. I'm watching them through the window from outside [the curtains were open] and the girl to whom she's talking is about 5 feet 4 inches tall, with light red hair down to her shoulders and she has a roundish, slightly freckled face." While this was going on McIntosh asked Sarah, one of the people present, to go up to Paula's room. A couple of minutes later Ann announced that she could see someone coming into Paula's room and gave a full description of Sarah. "Oh, it's Sarah!" She appeared surprised since she believed her to be in the room with Alistair McIntosh. "All three of them are killing themselves with laughter! They're in hysterics!" A few minutes later Sarah returned to the room with Paula and a red-haired girl, Jill, who fully fitted the description given by Ann. She confirmed that Ann had not met her and that they had all dissolved into laughter in Paula's room when Sarah had burst in and gone into fits of giggling on seeing Jill.

This astonishing piece of veridical information contains one small error. In her study Celia Green notes that "Deviations from complete accuracy in reproducing the normal world are more often reported in connection with experimental than with involuntary ecsomatic experiences (OOBEs)." The lack of accuracy in perception during OOBEs may lead one to suspect that the experience is not ecsomatic but clairvoyant in the way of the remote viewing experiment.

Alistair McIntosh's next step was to see if this clairvoyant

101

mediumship could be built up. Ann (his best subject) saw "guides" in the room and conveyed information which they imparted to her, regarding the nature of reality ("We are like bees in a hive building honey"). This "being" was full of light and of a higher spiritual plane. Interestingly Ann did not have recall during this "trance" episode and the views expounded were at variance with her own agnosticism at the time. On another occasion she was induced into trance and "controlled" by something which spoke a few words of an unknown language in a deep voice, then she woke up. McIntosh did not develop this "control" side of the experiment but instead went on to investigate the transcendent states which were attainable. By playing what he called "transcendental music" (Moody Blues and Oldfield's "Ommadawn") and telling the subject to raise her level of consciousness, he began to get descriptions from her of auras surrounding people and of a "silver chord" which attached her centre of awareness to her physical body or *soma*. These facets are common in accounts of mystical states and of OOBEs. The subjects found the experience exhilarating and immensely beneficial. They agreed with Blake's phrase that "the doors of perception were cleansed". The more eccentric by-products of psi-ability were passed over in pursuit of peak experiences of the kind which individuals usually find have a positive effect on mental health for a long time afterwards and which have been variously termed self-realisation, actualisation, integration, individuation. Alistair McIntosh evaluates his Christos experiments thus:

> The forehead massage acts as a particularly compelling stimulus on which the subject is forced to concentrate. Being far more potent than any form of mantra repetition or whatever, I therefore conclude that the Christos technique is basically a powerful deautomatizing technique. It enables good subjects to break down their normal restrictively structured consciousness and then using the lucid dream and the OOBE as a stepping stone, to experience their selves and reality at a different and perhaps more true level, as peak and mystical ASCs are entered.

Alistair McIntosh draws on the work of Robert Crookall

whose three books on Astral Projection were published in the early 1960s. He identifies four states.

(1) The Physical body — the "mortal coil" associated with a normal state of consciousness.
(2) The Vehicle of Vitality — sometimes seen as an aura and possibly biologically linked.
(3) The Psychical Body — vehicle for OOBEs and d-ASC.
(4) The Transcendent Mind — realised in peak and mystic states; Transpersonal consciousness (TC); samadhi/nirvana.

Crookall says that the extent to which categories (2) and (3) are mixed depends on whether the OOBE is natural or enforced. And while she might not agree with his terminology, Green's survey seems to bear this out, with her subclassification of "parasomatic" and "asomatic". But there is no proof that these four states are discrete entities and one can get bogged down in fancy words which attempt to ascribe sense data to something which is essentially non-sensual. Psychologists, psychiatrists and theologians are beginning to agree that there is such a thing as a "Higher State of Consciousness". Arthur Ludwig identifies ten characteristics of this "Altered State of Consciousness", such as a sense of timelessness and the ineffable, in a book of the same name. These would be asserted by mystics and Christos travellers (and presumably *clear* Scientologists).

There is much literature on mysticism which would be tedious to recount, for the essence of mysticism is *experiential*. But if it is read in conjunction with books on psychology and psychiatry we begin to see that there is a spectrum of such experience ranging from the Yoga samadhi, at one end, to the LSD-induced pseudo-psychosis of the acid-tripper at the other. In the middle is normal consciousness (NSC). Another fact which emerges is that one end is very different from the other despite the gradual spectrum in between. I cannot agree with Bertrand Russell that "from a scientific point of view we can make no distinction between the man who eats little and sees heaven and the man who drinks too much and sees snakes".

There is a very great difference between the alcoholic and the mystic. First, the former is operating at a lower level of consciousness which is impaired, while the latter is operating at a "supernormal" mode of perception while having all the other modes available to him. Russell is assuming that normal consciousness is the only mode of perceiving *fact*. Second, the "snakes" of the DTs sufferer cannot be verified by another witness (even if he is in DTs he will not see the same snakes because they are hallucinations). Whereas consensual validation (or confirmation) of the mystic's reality is shown in similar accounts of the transcendent experience. William James remarks in his Gifford Lectures: "Mystical states are absolutely authoritative over those who have them (although the outsider has not a duty to accept them uncritically), but they show the NSC to be only one kind, and open out other orders of truth."

This may seem to have drifted far from the subject of reincarnation. However, it is relevant in that it shows that much of "past lives" data are themselves a drift from NSC to ASC. If we stop at Glaskin then we are tempted to accept the data as evidence of reincarnation. But if we "drift" on to Transcendent States such as McIntosh achieved we begin to see the d-ASC and the OOBE as clairvoyant modes in which transpersonal consciousness (TC) and information is available.

Chapter 5

Survival—Does it Matter?

Albert Best would not thank me for telling you his address. It is a tenement flat in Glasgow which he keeps as a refuge from his travels as a clairvoyant medium at Spiritualist meetings in Britain and, on occasion, in Sweden, Rhodesia and South Africa. That makes him sound very "high-powered". As a medium he is the most powerful I have met, but he is far from high-powered in his lifestyle. Impish and Irish, he smiles at himself and the excesses of the Spiritualist movement in that particularly dry way characteristic of the Northern Irish. He is superintendent of a Glasgow Spiritualist Church and does only a few house sittings for which he refuses to take money. That is one reason he likes to keep his home address quiet. The other is that after his last television appearance he was telephoned by a religious crank who told him that his work was "of the Devil". Having myself been dignified in a similar way by one of the more extreme fundamentalist evangelicals in the Church of Scotland ministry, I can sympathise.

However, Albert Best has a fine literary testimony from another Church of Scotland minister, the Rev. David Kennedy of Lanark. Mr Kennedy's first wife died and while he was a widower he received a remarkable series of messages from her through Albert Best, who was known to them both before her death. Ann Kennedy — if she was the source of the messages — appeared to be concerned to give proof to her husband of her continuing existence.

Accordingly she "impressed" Best on a number of occasions (since her husband was not a "sensitive") and, using him as a go-between, was able to provide David Kennedy with the evidence which he has recorded in *A Venture in Immortality*.

105

The evidence is mostly of a trivial kind, but Kennedy feels that this is often the best. For example, the phone would ring and it would be Best. "Your wife wants to thank you for the two red roses that you put in front of her photograph." This was indeed accurate and known only to Kennedy. He had also voted Conservative at the General Election, having been a life-long socialist: Ann conveyed a teasing message. Both these instances could be explained by telepathy, but in the same session Best gave Kennedy a warning that there was a dangerous fault with his car lights. He went outside and checked them and found a side light was not working and was causing overheating in the wire. Trivial, but convincing to Kennedy. He writes of that session:

> Thus ended one of the best and most evidential episodes with Albert Best. The critic may choose to explain one item or even two as fraud or coincidence. Yet all together there are ten items of separate evidence contained in this session, and at the same session Albert was literally throwing "messages" to others in the group of ten people there. It seems to me that no theory of conscious or unconscious collecting of items concerning the people at this session could be conceived. The knowledge of the defect in the electrical system of my car leaves me with the problem of how even a discarnate entity can be aware of this. Nevertheless it happens.

David Kennedy now often appears in support of Albert Best and gives an address before Best's public demonstration of clairvoyance. He confesses that he started believing in survival and hoped for evidence. He acknowledges that he has sat with mediums who gave a hotch-potch of names, sometimes flannelling in a self-conscious and fraudulent way. That is often the experience of sincere sitters who go in pursuit of conclusive evidence at their first seance. Kennedy found his evidence in six months. Some people never find the proof they are looking for, but many who are lucky enough to have a sitting with Albert Best do.

Through a Glass, Barclay.

I have been to one of Best's public meetings and seen him identify a young girl in the audience and tell her the name and details of her newly dead husband. I have heard him pick out a family from South Africa, previously unknown to him, and give names of their friends back home. All along, the standard of accuracy is high and his delivery is good-humoured.

"There's a message for a lady at the back called Peggy, from her husband. Tell her not to bother about the milk and come and speak to him."

"That's right," shouted a lady. "Peg's gone to get milk for the tea." The *apres-seance* cup of tea is a feature of all such meetings when the medium can be thanked for messages he has been given.

Best's own moment of supreme proof was in Bulawayo when a Mashona witch-doctor called him into his hut, materialised his wife and three children, killed in the last war by an air-raid, and he conversed with them for a quarter of an hour. Materialisation mediums were more numerous in the Spiritualist movement in former times than nowadays. "If they've had a psychic experience," says Best, "they all think they are mediums — and there is a great difference. Most of them won't spend the time training to be a medium. That takes a long time, especially for materialisation. And healing . . ." — he rolls his eyes — "They all think they can heal."

In one sense Best might seem to be echoing the rivalry and backbiting which seems to bedevil spiritualism and those who have psychic gifts. However, if the implication is that he himself is better or different, he is right, as I learned personally.

My private sitting was recorded on cassette and I have listened to it a number of times. There are still names and details which I want to check further so I will only recount the main features. When I went to see him, the only thing Albert Best knew about me was that I worked for the BBC in Religious Broadcasting. The "patriarch" of BBC religious programmes in Scotland for the period 1950-70 had been the Rev. Dr Ronald Falconer and the outstanding "prophet" had been the Rev. Professor William Barclay. Both these men had died in the preceding year (Professor Barclay a matter of months previously), and I had a great personal affection and respect for both. So it is conceivable that if Albert had wanted to concoct a message he could not have chosen better than these two. If so, he might have gone and looked up details about them both. That must be said, yet I cannot personally believe this for two reasons. No one I have spoken to about him has other than a high opinion of the genuineness of his medium-ship; at the same time, some of the details he supplied would have required a great deal of research to acquire. Having said that I will now list what emerged from the sitting:

> *R. H. W. Falconer:* New Zealand origins, wife Bett and son Marshall. House in Terregles Road, Glasgow. Previously lived in Curour Road,Glasgow.(*) Stewart Lamont "following in his footsteps" i.e. in BBC Religious Broadcasting. Former assistant, Maggi, has ring with stone missing.(*) Close friend of Professor Barclay who is with him. *Professor Barclay:* recently passed over, tightness round chest.

Professor Barclay was a chronic bronchial patient. There followed lists of neighbours of the former houses of the Barclays and Falconers (which I have yet to trace) which were given as "evidence".

Even if I have not identified the names of the neighbours, the sitting yielded two remarkable pieces of information, marked (*). Neither of these pieces of information was known to me at the time but both were borne out later. Thus there was no possibility that Best could have gleaned them from me telepathically. I was forced to the conclusion that either Best had practised an elaborate fraud or he possessed a remarkable talent for mediumship. It was as simple as that and I was inclined to the latter view. But as we shall see, the matter is not that simple.

Albert Best worked for many years as a postman and the propensity to remember names in a street seems to affect his spirit communications. (This is a reason, as we shall see below, for wondering if the medium unintentionally colours the message on occasion by his own tastes, dispositions and memories.)

Out of the Frying Pan, Into the Fire.

If you cannot accept that reincarnation occurs, it does not mean that the evidence in favour of it is false or hallucinatory. There are alternative explanations. One has already been discussed: clairvoyance. Another is that the surviving spirits of people who previously lived still exist, and are available in certain circumstances to impart information. Reincarnation would then be possible if there is survival; or alternatively survival would explain reincarnation cases as mediumship exercised on those surviving spirits. Out-of-body experiences offer an interesting example of the "real self" being something which can detach itself from physical existence, perhaps survive the physical body, and perhaps reincarnate again. It is sometimes argued that if it is possible to establish that a discrete entity (spirit/soul/astral body) exists separately from the human body and carries intelligent information, then this would establish survival of death. But here care must be exercised, for out-of-body states during life might be inextricably linked to and dependent on the physical body, and would not necessarily survive bodily death.

This might be a sixth sense, as much part of the body as the eye or the ear. As we have already seen, OOBEs appear to be more common than we might imagine and they are capable of induction by various techniques. Dean Shiels has made a cross-cultural study of OOBEs in seventy non-Western cultures and concludes:

> Three conventional explanations of OOBEs belief (social control; crisis; and dream theories) were tested and found to be inadequate as explanations. . . . The near universality of OOBE and the consistency of the beliefs is striking . . . in comparing the OOBE beliefs of the cultures with modern OOBE there are many points of agreement.

This study may, if it does nothing else, illustrate that whatever an OOBE is, it is a part of man's psychical nature and not a product of social, personal, psychological or religious factors. But the importance of the OOBE lies in helping to establish the idea that something which exists separately from the human body and carries intelligent information, could survive death.

Deathbed Testimony

Resuscitation techniques in hospitals have made the occurrence of "near-to-death" experiences more common. These often take the form of OOBEs. There is a feeling of peace, transcendence; often a strong "light" is experienced, together with an increased ability to recall past memories; often this is accompanied by sensory observation of people in the room during loss of consciousness. Dr Raymond Moody, in his book *Life After Life*, has assembled an interesting set of such accounts and has more recently followed it with *Reflections on Life After Life*. His approach is not that of a parapsychologist but that of a medical man and is thus interesting for the clinical and practical light he sheds. The patients he spoke to often no longer feared death after their OOBE experience. Occasionally religious figures intrude — people report being greeted by a guiding light, an angel (or a Jesus figure) who comforts them. A parallel study to Moody's has recently been written by Grof and Hamilton in *The Human Encounter With Death*. They examine the effect of the drug LSD on cancer patients and bear out the Moody pattern of "going down a tunnel" into light. They describe it as a kind of para-natal experience of Death-Birth.

Moody cites a number of instances of such experiences from ancient literature, among them Plato, the Bible, the Venerable Bede and De Quincey. The Jungian psychologist might say that what is described are universal symbols, the tunnel, the angel of light, and so on. That does not mean that the symbols do not signify a state that is as "real" as normal consciousness, but in which "the doors of perception are cleansed". For he found that of all the patients who had had such a deathbed experience and revivied, none still feared death and all of them, far from treating the experience as a dream, regarded it as a personal proof of survival. Often present with the experience was a panoramic recall of the important events of the individual's life — this took place in seconds of actual time, yet somehow the time-scale was frozen. One subject who had such an experience during a cardiac arrest reported that as he reached the end of the panoramic review the figures he observed round his bed were frozen in a "still-frame" like a movie, before being jolted into action again as he recovered consciousness. Most of the subjects felt that during this review they became conscious of how parts of their life had been worthy/unworthy. In other words, they "judged" themselves.

In his book *You Cannot Die*, Ian Currie lists some examples of his own. Interestingly his examples and those of Moody often arise from a shock to the physical body, which triggers the experience, a cardiac arrest for example, a shotgun wound, or a car crash. Recently I heard the account of one man who had such an experience when accidentally borne aloft clutching the tail-plane of an aircraft during the war. The plane flew across the chilly waters off Orkney and landed in soft snow, which enabled him to live and tell the tale. Most of these examples are anonymous because they come from medical sources, but one factor which emerges is their remarkable corroboration with one another. One subtle criticism which might be levelled against the results is that too many of the subjects have read about near-death experiences, but since there has been very little published on the subject until recently this criticism can be discounted. However, widespread coverage of Dr Elizabeth Kubler-Ross's work with terminal patients and of Moody's findings, will give more force to this argument in the future.

The widespread use of drugs with terminal patients must also raise the question of whether the experience is hallucinatory. It is well known that hallucinations can have a pathological basis, both organic and biochemical. This can be due to sensory deprivation; chemical effects of psycho-pharmacological products; anatomical brain lesions and endogenous psychoses; REM sleep suppression; or to oxygen deficiency.

Since many of Kubler-Ross and Moody's patients were drugged, and Gorf and Hamilton's were purposefully under LSD, we must be careful to assess their experience with this in mind. But another study has recently come on the scene by Karlis Osis of the USA and by the Icelandic parapsychologist Erlendur Haraldsson. Entitled *At the Hour of Death*, it describes surveys of what doctors and nurses observed in patients as they approached death. Their basic contention is that a majority of apparition phenomena in the dying cannot be explained medically.

In reviewing the book, Dr James McHarg points out that although they exclude four or five medical possibilities, they miss out the most likely of all — transitory cerebral anoxia (oxygen deficiency) which he states is a well-known cause of visual hallucination. He points out that a predisposition to temporal lobe disturbances in the brain may well have a much larger incidence in the general population than is suspected at present. Hence hallucination of figures on deathbeds, after-death states or OOBEs in which the percipient "escapes" his painful condition, are to be expected. However, Dr McHarg

111

concedes that by discounting a medical factor, Osis and Haraldsson deprive themselves of a tool which would be useful to their argument, namely that the ESP from the deceased which they claim to have discovered in the patients may well be facilitated by such transitory disturbance of brain function. Put more crudely, this means that even if a schizophrenic patient is insane, his very insanity may enable him to see paranormal phenomena as well as his "normal" hallucinations. But sorting out the paranormal monkeys from the schizophrenic trees is hardly going to be easy!

So we ought to return to more conventional OOBEs which may demonstrate the possibility of OOBE without the presence of drugs or psychiatric ailments. Celia Green's study (mentioned previously) is interesting in this regard. She has shown that a wide variety of people experience OOBEs, that these are linked with relaxed states and that they usually involve one sense (sight). She also points out that deviations from accuracy in reproducing the normal environment are sometimes present. For example one percipient saw a chimney stack in an OOBE which was not present in the actual environment. Also there is often an ESP element present.

> I looked down at my body then kind of floated out of the room into some street I didn't know and stopped before a house and I entered and went to a bedroom facing the stairs. The man lying in bed was a very old friend of mine whom I had not seen for a year or two. I met him about six or seven months later and he said he had moved to a new district. When I told him he lived in an upstairs flat and how the furniture was placed in the bedroom, he wanted to know how I knew.

ESP could explain why details which could not otherwise be perceived are available to the percipient. The minor inaccuracies might point to some kind of clairvoyance at work such as occurs in the "Mindreach" or the Remote Veiwing of Targ and Puthoff.

But if the OOBE is an imagined experience (i.e. not an actual detachment from the body), then a target could be set up, to be viewed during the OOBE, which looked different depending on the position of the observer. For example, a target is placed behind a window and "distorted" by mirrors and colour filters. From a viewpoint in front of the window it appears as one thing, while in reality it is very different. Karlis Osis used this technique with Ingo Swann, Alex Tanous and a gentleman with the colourful name of Blue Harary, but the results were open to different interpretations. Objections were advanced, that even the "distortion" could be circumvented by the wiles of psi, so that the value of setting up such a complex task was negated. Alternatively it is argued that if an OOBE observer was to see the distorted image, which appeared in the same form as to an ordinary observer, this would imply some kind of eye in the OOBE state which bent light into a focused picture. This "third eye" is presumably contained in the astral body which OOBE enthusiasts claim travels out of the physical body.

The two theories, one, that during an OOBE "something" detaches from the physical body and, two, that an OOBE is a "fantasy-construct" using ESP, are not mutually exclusive. Karlis Osis is now prepared to blend the two theories. He set up further experiments with Blue Harary and the best results were obtained when Harary tried to "travel" to a target room, using his cat to detect his presence when he arrived in the room. These experiments lend strength to the idea that information acquired during an OOBE is not just imagination or clairvoyance but that "something" can detach from the physical body.

A number of other theories have been advanced by various astral travellers, among them Robert Munroe, Robert Crookall, Sylvan Muldoon and Hereward Carrington. Their argument is mostly in favour of the "astral" body hypothesis which often appears "clothed" and linked to the body by a "silver cord". This has caused fierce debate and the enthusiasts have countered that the astral body is a symbolisation of the self to the self, and that both it and the cord are constructed by the mind in order to allay anxiety at being apparently without a body. This can be turned around to imply that if the mind can construct such an astral body, it can construct the whole experience using ESP. Sue Blackmore, in her useful pamphlet, *Parapsychology and OOBEs*, published by the SPR in November 1978, points out that errors in the observed world during OOBEs are usually additions to the real environment: she explains OOBEs as memory-constructs combined with dreams.

Celia Green, however, contends that such errors are more often reported in OOBEs done under experimental conditions where relaxed states lead to the imagination taking flight, than in the involuntary experiences. Both Green, and Muldoon and Carrington cite cases where the OOBE subject has been observed at the target location. Ms Blackmore is sceptical of the theory that an entity leaves the body or even that ESP is at work during OOBEs as a construction from memory and tends, although she does not use the term, to think of an OOBE as an *induced lucid dream*. She comes down strongly on the side of non-paranormal explanations, but appears to ignore the spontaneous cases furnishing information which could not have come from memory.

There is a marked division between the Crookall school and Ms Blackmore's scepticism, with Celia Green and the Institute of Psychophysical Research somewhere in the middle. All we can conclude is that there are plenty of facts, a few theories, but no agreement, and that while the OOBE does not provide proof of survival, there are indications that it may be possible.

Transpersonal Consciousness (TC)

This somewhat daunting term is used by the distinguished parapsychologist W. E. Roll in his contributions to *New Directions in Parapsychology*. He argues that in OOBEs the field of consciousness is limited to the familiar four-dimensional world of human personality, whereas in TC the field of consciousness is all-embracing. OOBEs offer evidence of information acquired paranormally, whereas the TC is more akin to mystical experience. However, says Roll, the fact that consciousness can extend beyond the physical organism of the body is not to say that it exists apart from it. Nor is it correct to say that survival of consciousness implies survival of personality.

Indeed consciousness and personality are two distinct and different things. C. D. Broad defines consciousness as resulting from interaction between a person and his environment. If the sensory stimuli are removed from a person's immediate environment he will fall asleep. If sensory stimuli are removed from within his brain, he will not dream. So, it is argued, the component of mind which might survive independent of the brain substrata is *unconscious*. Consciousness can exist without any of the components of

114

personality (which are linked to body type, brain capacity and inherited capacity, as well as acquired skill and experience). Indeed the more "detached" a person becomes from the leaden feet of his personality (both his ballast and his handicap), the greater is his awareness. When perception, memories and emotions from the past are transcended, then awareness becomes more vivid and rich. Such mystical states are the stuff of TC. Roll puts forward the idea of a different level of consciousness which persists after an organism dies. He calls it theta-consciousness.

> If transpersonal consciousness represents the after death state (at least for some people at some time) this might help us understand some of the peculiarities in the survival data. If the memories, dispositions and skills of the deceased do not necessarily belong to the consciousness associated with them in life, but can be activated by others, the confusion of memories and personal identity so common in mediumship studies is easy to understand.

In other words, our individual stream of consciousness merges into an ocean of collective consciousness whose waters are sometimes muddied, and occasionally clear. The clairvoyant is the pearl-fisher whose keen eye picks out experiences from our individual lives. It is an interesting theory and it brings us neatly to the critical question.

Do We Survive Death?

At first asking, the question is a simple one. But on closer inspection, these four short words have introduced a number of confusing puzzles. What is "death"? It is all very well to point to absence of heartbeats or of brainwaves and define death in either or both of these terms. But just as the decomposing corpse in the grave mixes with the soil around, it is possible that some of the content of the psyche mixes with a collective or racial memory in which fragments of personal experience and memory are preserved. Are we then dead and does this count as survival? If it does not, then what part of us must persist after physical death for us to be able to claim we have survived?

Even the use of the first person plural, "we", begs another question. Is it "I" who survives or bits of "us" in a suprapersonal state? Looking at the evidence for survival with these questions in mind should make for a more perceptive analysis. However, the evidence itself is far from being straightforward. If you are tempted to say, "Surely we survive death or we don't?", then you are unlikely to get very far and likely to end up confused.

As we have already seen, looking at poltergeists, there is an apparent intelligence behind many of the phenomena, like the cushions with the same dimensions as drawers which wore substituted in a sideboard in the Grieve house in Springburn. This "intelligence" appears to be mediated through a person or persons or derived from them. Yet most poltergeist investigators would not say they are dealing with "dead spirits" or an entity which has a "life" of its own. Thus the entity called a poltergeist is perhaps an artefact — a "do-it-yourself-without-consciously-trying" spirit which has been conjured up. The implication is that much survival evidence is a combination of telepathy and PK, such as the poltergeist. When it comes to mediums, a mature personality, not an adolescent one, is writing the script.

Another difficulty is raised by the EVP. So ambiguous is the evidence here that the prime investigators are divided as to whether it consists of coherent patterns imposed on random noise; discarnate or dead spirits communicating; intelligent life from another planet getting in touch; or PK exercised by the experimenter on the tape; or even akin to forms of poltergeist activity like the Enfield "voices".

It does not matter whether you are firmly convinced by one of these explanations: the fact remains that no one has conclusively shown the EVP to be one of them. Thus if electronic signals have been captured by tape which are not proved to be from "dead people" then how many other "mediumistic" messages from "beyond the grave" are similarly mis-identified?

The next area of concern is spiritualism. Despite being in existence for nearly a century, this religious movement has not produced a great deal of startling evidence. This is because much of the information communicated at seances is of a trivial nature ("Tell Aunt Jessie that she's to be careful coming down stairs"), and leads some critics to say that if this kind of stuff is all that the dead are concerned with, they would rather not survive. But even if it is trivial, much of the spiritualist evidence is very explicit. The dead describe green fields and people in long, white robes. The difficulty is that much of the sensory reality in this world is conditioned by its physical nature. Fields are green because that is the section of the visible spectrum in which they reflect light; the blades of grass in the field are a structured part of the carbon-oxygen cycle known as photosynthesis. We perceive them with eyes which are set in bodies which need to be clothed (in white robes?) to protect us from excesses of temperature and/or revealing reproductive organs around which the human animal has evolved modest rituals. The irony is immediate — why clothes or indeed bodies, in a world that need not have our evolution patterns? Why grass, when it is botanically rooted in our type of planet? The more subtle apologist for spiritualism will say that the fields and robes are mythical and only put forward as categories of explanation to humans who cannot conceive of a non-physical world. However, that is not how it comes across in spiritualist literature.

The spiritualist philosophy is a kind of dualism of spirit and matter. The "spirit" is something set over against matter and at death the soul leaves its tomb (*sema*) in the body (*soma*). This word-play of *soma-sema* in Greek was made much of by the Gnostics who believed in an evolutionary progress of the soul to various degrees of knowledge (gnosis), just as the spiritualists believe in a kind of progress of the soul after death.

It is easy to see how this view received sympathy in the closing years of the last century, when classical materialist views of the universe were gaining ground and matter was seen as a collection of billiard balls. Spirit, it followed, was not solid but "ethereal". However, it goes against the whole thrust of modern physics to see matter in this way and it is difficult to see how spiritualists would explain the interaction of spirit and matter to produce PK effects. Crude attempts to do so in the works of J. Arthur Findlay postulate "ether" and ectoplasm as a halfway-house between spirit and matter. The Michelson-Morley experiment put paid to such ether theories and they are rarely now resuscitated. More recently, the Australian physicist Raynor C. Johnson tried to do so but it is doubtful whether his theories differ much from speculation as to whether pigs can fly.

Both Johnson and Findlay look for explanations in terms of the electromagnetic (e/m) spectrum, as if making contact with the other world was only a case of turning to the right spot on the dial. If this were the case, with the advance of electronic equipment, there would be more knowledge about such a world. But the reverse has happened. Spiritualist gnosis is on the decline. "We have the only religion and philosophy based on scientifically-proved phenomena," stated an article on 27 May 1978, in the *Psychic News*, the newspaper of the spiritualist movement. But most of the spiritualist evidence is not "scientific" and very few of the scientists working in the field are interested in it. There has been a decline in physical mediumship in recent years — some would say, cynically, because of the increased means of detecting fraud in darkened seance rooms by infra-red photography.

The spiritualist movement received a setback in 1978 when the spiritualists' National Association President, Gordon Higginson, was accused of cheating at a meeting in which he gave the names of several people which also appeared on a sheet of paper in the anteroom he had occupied before the meeting. But even if spiritualism is the music hall of psychic phenomena, it is turning up phenomena of at least passing interest at a steady rate. Maurice Barbanell, who started *Psychic News* in 1932 with the late Hannen Swaffer, told me: "I don't accept things . . . we sift material day by day. You might explain any one facet on its own but the evidence is cumulative." As for some of the attempts to discredit evidence supplied by mediums, he says: "Sometimes the explanations are more fantastic than the facts."

Interestingly, one set of evidence of survival which most spiritualists do not accept is reincarnation. They would prefer to suggest that the second-time-around person is being given the details of his past life by the spirit of a person who has already lived on earth and is now in the "after-life". They may even concede that the spirit-guide of the person who claims reincarnation is exercising a continual mediumship through them, so that the memories and personality of a long dead person constitute a second self. But if, as the spiritualists believe, survival does not imply reincarnation, reincarnation does not necessarily imply personal survival. As we have seen, some form of clairvoyance may be at work, supplying information to the "reincarnated" person. However, even if the evidence for reincarnation were proved beyond peradventure, then it still means the "real" world is the sensory world of flesh and blood on earth, because it is to this world that the discarnate soul returns. If another immortal world does not exist, why does the soul bother coming back and not stay in its "long home"? Usually the answer given is the principle of Karma — the recycling of souls until they achieve the moral perfection or expiation of sin to progress. No doubt I shall incur another Karma for thinking this naughty thought, but I don't understand why if the next world is so enlightened, they can't do the job over there or even go on strike and stay where it's nicer.

The whole matter is complicated by the "medium" through which the information is passed. When a spiritualist medium passes information it is often "coloured" by his or her own perceptions. This leads some to shout "fraud", but we must be fair in this regard. Consider the party game "Chinese Whispers", in which a message is whispered from person to person and is inevitably distorted en route, often with amusing consequences. Could not many mediumistic communications fall into the same category? If Raudive imposed certain interpretations on his taped EVP voices, then it still might be possible that they were genuine voices not just noise, and that only his interpretation was wrong.

This still does not solve the fundamental question. This is not "Is the evidence correct?" but "Where did this message originate?". If the source was some clairvoyant capacity of the medium to pick up information in the way that a homing pigeon "knows" its way home, then we are certainly no nearer to proving survival. If it was some dissociated aspect of the medium's personality (seen in its most acute form in schizophrenic conditions), then we cannot say that any discarnate entity exists. This is known in psychical research as the "Telephone Problem" — how do we really know the identity of the person speaking to us? Impersonations, frauds and hallucinations, notwithstanding, it is not easy to say definitely that survival is proved unless the evidence is outstanding. In all of this, the filtering effect of the medium does not help.

There are a few great physical mediums today like D. D. Home and Eusapio Palladino, but there is quite a variety of

119

mediumship ranging from the upturned wine glass and the Ouija board so beloved of students looking for a supernatural thrill, to the idiosyncratic mediumship of Rosemary Brown who "composes" music under the direction of dead composers like Chopin, Liszt and Stravinsky, often with a gripping degree of verisimilitude.

Although not musically trained myself, when I visited Mrs Brown's Wimbledon home I had the advantage of a previous conversation with a music critic and had a ounning question in mind. The following is a shortened version of an interview in which I began by asking her what sort of musical training she had had before receiving these communications.

Mrs Brown Well, I've had very little musical training — this has been checked on many times of course, and also as a child I heard very little music: we were a very, very poor family and we couldn't go to concerts and have records and so on.

S. Lamont What sort of proof could you offer that it's not imitation, a very clever craft that you have, of imitating famous styles?

Mrs Brown A lot of musicologists have said, you know, the volume of music and the variety of styles in itself is enough to be convincing. Nobody could keep on turning out music in so many different styles, with all the characteristics. Apart from that there are instances which rule out the idea of imitation. One of the best and most recent instances is the case of Victor Ullman who was a Czech Jew and he composed an opera while he was in a concentration camp and the opera was smuggled out of the camp and eventually arrived in London and of course I'd never heard of Victor Ullman — I don't suppose many people have at all, other than the privileged few who've got to hear of this opera, and I was met at one time by a man whose name was Kerry Woodward — he used to work for the BBC, he now works in Holland — and he eventually became cognisant of this opera. He met the man into whose possession the opera had come and when Kerry Woodward met me, the late Victor Ullman appeared. Of course I didn't know who he was, I'd never seen anybody like it before and he gave me his name and I thought with a name like Ullman he was probably German, and Liszt, who was also German, interrupted and said 'No, he's of Slav blood'. Obviously I can't remember all the wealth of detail that came from Victor Ullman, but he began talking about the opera which I could not possibly have seen and he talked in great detail about it, naming bar numbers and what he'd written on a certain page. It couldn't possibly have come out of my subconscious mind. It wasn't there in my subconscious mind — it's extraordinary.

SL   Is it possible that if Liszt is there just now, he actually would be able to give answers to questions I might give?

Mrs B   Well sometimes he can, sometimes other composers have done this. Debussy did this with Richard Rodney Bennett.

SL   For instance there's a work of Liszt's, a religious work which he wrote late in his career, called "Via Concis", which is a very beautiful work and some conductors might have difficulty with, say, whether it should be played with muted strings or not, now . . .

Mrs B   Yes, yes. [pause] No he says, not with muted strings, they should be quiet but not too muted to get the right balance — they must not be muted.

SL   Why is it mostly piano pieces that you have composed — because that's your own instrument? Or are there never any orchestrals?

Mrs B   Oh there are orchestra works and string quartets and pieces for violin and piano and so on. I suppose there's more piano music because it's easier to transmit a piece of piano music rather than a full orchestral score.

Feeling somewhat ashamed of having misled "Liszt", even if it was in the interests of psychic research, I journeyed to

Berkhamstead, to the picturesque home of Antony Hopkins, whose analysis of music in words has few equals. He gave me his opinion of Rosemary Brown's works:

A. Hopkins   Well some of it I find very convincing and interesting, for example there's a Bagatelle allegedly by Beethoven which is an extremely good imitation of Beethoven, whatever else it may be, and I do find the whole story of the Ullman opera absolutely fascinating — to my mind that's far and away the most convincing bit of evidence that's been produced. I think it's partly because Ullman was alive much nearer to our present day and equally because there's no possibility of her ever having heard a note of his music, so therefore at any rate she was working out of complete darkness, so to speak. The whole story of that I find totally fascinating. When it comes to the pieces by what I call the greater masters, whether it's Brahms or Schubert or Beethoven or Liszt, or whoever, I find the cases much less convincing with regard to the quality of the music, because one would assume that these composers, after they have passed on, would become better not worse, whereas in fact what they're producing is music which is on the whole inferior to the music which they produced during their lives.

I rather more incline to the view that Mrs Brown may be dipping into a reservoir from which creative energy comes and doing so with a cup or bowl that is shaped in the style of Beethoven or Liszt. You see, that would explain why the music is really rather superficial, and repetitious.

SL   So in a sense it's not the actual person of Liszt standing there behind her shoulder?

AH   I feel not. As you know I prompted you to ask a question of Rosemary Brown and it was rather mean-minded of me to do this. But you see I've always felt that people ask the wrong questions and it would be very easy to ask a specific question which would give you

SL

AH

an absolute answer as to whether it was Liszt or not. Now the "Via Crucis" is a work which obviously Liszt would have very much taken to his heart. It's a profoundly religious work written towards the end of his life. It is written for chorus and organ and he would have played the organ parts himself — there is no orchestra and there are no strings, and so when one asks whether the strings should be played muted or not you're asking a trick question, to which unfortunately she gave an answer which gave us the impression that Liszt could not possibly actually be speaking to her.

Nonetheless, if the person of Liszt was not there standing at her shoulder the whole gamut of works that she has produced are somewhat remarkable in themselves. Would you agree?

Oh yes. Yes I wouldn't challenge that for one moment. I simply challenge the explanation and I feel that there are passages in these pieces of alleged Liszt for example that are so weak that he as a living composer would never have passed them. Whereas equally there are some passages which are resembling Liszt enough to make one feel, "well, there's certainly a whiff of authenticity there".

Not all spiritualist mediums produce evidence for survival which is pleasant on the ear. But the list of different types of evidence is varied:

Psychic Art. Drawing portraits of the dead communicated on a sketch pad. Has all the disadvantages of police identikits and it can be said that the medium uses the relative confronting her as a model.

Psychometry. "Sensing" of an object which belonged to a dead person and using it as a focus to give messages about them — e.g. grandfather's gold watch will furnish a picture of grandfather. But the object can just as easily belong to a living person and it is difficult to say that this is not clairvoyance muddied with survival presuppositions.

Direct Voice. Medium goes into trace and sitters hear

123

voices coming from elsewhere. Sometimes a tin trumpet or cone is used and this levitates and is "used" by the voice. Impressive, but usually mediums need a darkened room and this heightens difficulties of objective assessment.

Trance. Common in light form when the medium is aware of his "control" and surroundings. But his "Red Indian" voices are often coloured by his own local accent. Deep trance means the medium is unaware of what he says during control and can yield some startling personality changes and voices.

Clairaudience. A form of light trance in which the medium hears an "inner voice" giving him the information. He is aware of both control and client and talks between the two. One of the foremost is the Irish medium, Albert Best of Glasgow, who was discussed above and again later in this chapter.

Ectoplasm. This substance is extruded by a medium in deep trance and is said by spiritualists to be the clay through which they leave their otherwise invisible print. It emerges from the medium's ears, nose and navel and looks like poached egg-white or muslin cloth (the latter having been used to cheat the effect on a few occasions). In the transfiguration seance, the ectoplasm is believed to cling to the medium's features, which are then moulded and highlighted to reveal the identity of the controlling spirit.

A well-known exponent of this psychic art is Mrs Queenie Nixon: the effect is quite eerie and dramatic, but as in the case of a child shining a torch onto its chin, the image may not be ectoplasm but shadow. Mediums who can produce lifesized sculptures in ectoplasm are, like direct-voice mediums, now very scarce. Gordon Higginson, of the Spiritualists National Union, is claimed to do this, but was not willing to be filmed for our television series. This whole area is riven with controversy, since illusionists have been able to replicate the phenomenon easily.

Automatic Writing. This sometimes occurs through a planchette (a wooden palette on wheels with a pencil stuck through it) which writes out its messages. On other occasions light or deep trance is involved. Occasionally the writing has been identified as bearing a direct relationship to that of the alleged spirit when alive.

Ouija Board. A pointer on a wooden board with letters. These are not so common as they once were, but letters of the alphabet, pasted round a table on which an upturned wine glass is touched by the fingertips of the sitters, are an easy substitute.

These last two forms of mediumship are the most common among amateur mediums who often find they have opened a psychic sewer when the glass starts to spell out expletives. Spiritualists explain this as being due to the unprogressed "astral" spirits which are still clinging to an earthbound existence — murderers and suicides for example. The impressionable dabbler has been known to get a severe fright and become convinced that demons are at work. Like the poltergeist, the demon or devil relishes and exploits any subconscious fears in the sitters and this seems to release more energy for the phenomenon. In this context it is worth mentioning again Philip, the Imaginary Ghost "created" by Dr George Owen and friends. Is the fear father to the phantom, in other words? Spiritualists would say the reason that mediums do not get the "nasty" spirits, is that they have learned to repel such entities who attempt to control them or their guide (we all have one apparently) does it for them. Perhaps it is simply that they have learned which parts of their unconscious should be allowed to surface.

I would not like to imply that spiritualists are insincere or fraudulent. There are some extremely gifted psychics within their ranks. But in general, as a movement, they are still hung up on an outdated Victorian metaphysic and a totally outdated form of language, and cling to a Moodey and Sankey mission-hall atmosphere at their gatherings. They are sectarian in outlook, and the profusion of churches is testimony to the quarrelsome spirits (of the all-too-human kind) which are attracted to a situation where one psychic vies with another for the limelight. They are not as a movement noted for an over-abundance of leaders, speakers, or writers who are possessed with even an average abundance of literacy. In short, it is perhaps not surprising that a movement which firmly believes that it is a religion and spends most of its time seeking to contact the dead will not be taken seriously by the scientists and parapsychologists as having provided proof of survival. Having said that, and having eliminated the charlatans and self-deluding followers, it remains true that belief in survival provides hope and comfort for many bereaved people.

125

There is one other obstacle to accepting survival evidence at face value. It is supremely stated in the Gordon Davis case, as it appears in the *Proceedings* of the SPR, Vol. 35 (1925). The famous psychic researcher Dr A. C. Soal had sittings in 1921-22 with Mrs Blanche Cooper as medium. During these he conversed with a character (John Ferguson) invented by himself between sittings (his thoughts being picked up telepathically by Mrs Cooper), and with the "spirit" of an old schoolfriend, Gordon Davis, who had apparently died in the Great War. Davis described how he had lived in Brighton Some time later when walking there, to his astonishment Soal bumped into Gordon Davis, who was still very much alive. Soal checked the record of the seance, which was brief but detailed, and found that it contained information about Davis he could not have known (and thus transmitted to Mrs Cooper) and other information, such as his move to Brighton, which was not true at the time of the seance, but came true later! In the same series of sittings, Soal also appeared to be in contact with his dead brother, Frank. Clearly, if the other controls were not what they seemed to be, what of Frank? Could he not be a dramatised product of the medium's mind formed from information gained telepathically?

The introduction of telepathy does not explain things away. This is often known as the Super ESP Hypothesis which postulates that since nearly everything is known to someone somewhere (or will be), then by a judicious mix of telepathy, clairvoyance, precognition and postcognition, anything can be known through ESP. Thus, it is argued, there is no need for a spiritist or dualist hypothesis, when a simpler alternative is available. It is a matter of opinion which is the simpler explanation. Personally, I agree with Mr Barbanell in this case, that some of the outlandish explanations far exceed the hypothesis they seek to replace.

But the Gordon Davis case does raise some very serious questions for those who believe in survival. How many "dead" controls are really clairvoyant images from past, present and future? What fascinates me about this question is the implication that it contains assumptions about time which ought to be explored. I shall return to these presently. In the meantime, if spiritualism is the music hall of survival evidence, it is perhaps the moment to start looking at the calendar of concert-hall evidence as contained in the SPR files.

Sealed-Package Tests

Those patriarchs of psychical research, F. W. H. Myers and Sir Oliver Lodge, both left sealed packets with the SPR and intended to attempt to communicate their contents through a medium after their deaths. Neither succeeded, but even if they had, someone would no doubt have objected that the medium could have obtained the evidence clairvoyantly. More recently, two of their successors, Professor Ian Stevenson and Dr Robert Thouless, have devised an experiment to communicate the key of a cipher to a medium, which will then enable a passage to be read giving the content of the packet. Both these gentlemen are still alive at the time of writing and I wish them many more years before the experiment reaches its veridical stage.

Dr Thouless explained to me the reasons behind his macabre experiment:

> I thought it would be better to communicate something after my death that wasn't an object that a medium could be supposed to know by extra-sensory perception but was just the key to unlock a cipher. I've left in various places in my book, *From Anecdote to Experiment in Psychical Research*, and elsewhere, a passage in cipher. That is, it's a jumble of letters which convey the message if one knows how to interpret it. It's like the ciphers that are used in military communications for secret messages. It's been made according to some complicated rules but there are certain passages from literature or words which if they are conveyed will form the key to unlocking the cipher. Anybody who has that key will be able to get back the meaningful message with which I started and the evidence that they've got the right key is that it becomes a meaningful message. I, and I alone, know what the key is and I think if I can communicate it through a medium after my death, that would be very strong evidence that I am still existing as a stream of consciousness, as a mind. Not, as I've said, conclusive, but pointing that way very strongly. As far as the form that this survival might take, there are various possibilities. The Jewish-Christian tradition is of a reconstruction of a spiritual body at the time of the

resurrection. The question I think that's more interesting to most of us is whether we go on surviving as a stream of thought between the time of death and the time of resurrection and that's what I call continuing survival. Eh, it's very difficult to say whether the early Christians, for example, believed in that or not. I've read St Paul's Chapter in 2nd Corinthians many times and never discovered whether he thought that the dead person continued between his death and his resurrection or whether he didn't and I think if you'd asked St Paul, he'd have said "What does it matter?".

The Cross-Correspondences

F. W. H. Myers was the originator of this attempt to eliminate "telepathic leakage" of veridical information already known to the sitter, being picked up by the medium. Myers was a classical scholar, and literary allusions, clues and information meaningless in themselves were received after his death by several automatists as far apart as India, America and Britain, containing references to the other automatists and purporting to be from Myers or former SPR colleagues of his. Alice Johnson, one of the investigators, was the first to fit part of the puzzle together into a meaningful whole. The painstaking study occupies many pages of the *Proceedings* of the SPR over many years and when one of the original automatists, Mrs Winifred Coombe-Tennant (Mrs Willett) came through after her death to the medium, Geraldine Cummins, the whole fascinating tale took a new turn. This is written up in Ms Cummins' book, *Swan on a Black Sea*. Altogether it constitutes one of the most powerful pieces of evidence in favour of survival and against the Super ESP Hypothesis.

Known Only To The Dead

Fortunately the Cross Correspondences are not the only instances of mediums coming up with information they could not have "tapped" or cheated. There is the case of Edgar Vandy in which a boy who had accidentally drowned in a pool gave information supplementary to the post mortem carried out on his body. There is the Chaffin-Will case, in which a farmer had died, leaving his farm to his third son and his widow unprovided for. Chaffin came through and described where a second, more generous will would be found, after giving a clue in the pocket of an old coat. All the facts were subject to a court case and seem quite remarkable.

The third instance is quoted by Nils Jacobson in his book *Life Without Death?* of a man whose father had died in an accident in 1928. In a seance in 1934 the man was told, ostensibly by his father, that the cause of death was different from what he had always imagined, and on checking the hospital records, he found that this was indeed the case.

These three instances are not isolated or exceptionally rare. While it must be readily admitted that the psychic world is full of cranks, charlatans and credulous people, there is still a lot of authenticated evidence. I have not catalogued case after case, partly because the original accounts are there to be consulted by the interested reader, but also because in this particular area there are tremendous existential barriers to belief or disbelief. "Until I see the wounds in his hands and feet, I will not believe" (John 20, v. 25). "Though the dead be raised — they still will not believe" (Luke 16, v. 31).

There are incentives to believe in survival — positive thinking, wish-fulfilment — and if it could be conclusively shown that we do not survive, and that our three-score-years-and-ten of unequal struggle were the sum total of pleasure and meaningfulness which Providence sees fit to allot us, then I fear that the suicide rate and the admission rate to psychiatric wards would shoot up. But even if there is impressive evidence for survival, it is not conclusive. That is why it is an *existential* question.

How we approach that question may itself determine not just the answer we give — but even the outcome as far as we are concerned. The Tibetan Book of the Dead seems to suggest that the type of after-life we inhabit may to some extent be determined by our expectations and aspirations. That is to say that those who crave a never-ending sex orgy will inevitably receive it. I prefer to think of the parable of Hell as a banqueting hall groaning with delights, while the inhabitants are tormented by only having twelve-foot spoons to eat with; meanwhile Heaven has exactly the same set-up, except the inhabitants feed each other with the twelve-foot spoons! That is not just a tale with a moral. It also contains the theological thought that there is not a dualist divide between Heaven and Hell or between Spirit and Maker. We inhabit both worlds simultaneously.

Modern theologians are often thought to be "soft" on Hell

because they define it as being "out of the presence of God". But paradoxically the worst pain is the absence of feeling, not the sharp spasm which reminds us of pleasures lost. If we consider this meaningless abyss of frozen time where all roads lead nowhere and no one cares about anyone else, I think we have the recipe for the most horrific state of personal darkness. What then is Heaven? It is the same person standing in the *same place* but with purpose; time is rolling past, you are moving towards people and they towards you. It is dynamic, not static. Heaven and Hell are the same carousel, one in motion, the other stopped. The difference is one of life or death.

The question of time is all important here. We cannot conceive of immortality, because we cannot conceive of infinity and we are experiencing the world in finite, brief quantities of time; ebbing seconds in a sand-glass; the pulsing beat of body clocks running down into death; cycles of light and darkness; periods of sleep and wakefulness; seasons of birth and decay. We cannot stand still because we are constantly moving. So there is no possibility of jumping off the carousel to see how fast we are moving relative to the absolute. Thus we can only see and hear now. What is past is memory. We might see what is to come if we could step outside the body clock which measures out life in seconds, into an existence where time present and time past are both contained in time future.

But even if we could step off the carousel, who could tell the difference between a memory and a premonition and the experience of a moment? The first is stored in the brain. The second has yet to be, and has no reality except as an hallucination. The third is apprehended at the present moment. It melts in the mind and is gone, into the past and the drawers marked "memory". To the outside observer — the absolute observer — memory and telepathy and immediate experience would be one, fused reality. Such an observer would not be time-conditioned, thus past and future would mean as much as present. So we would die and yet live. We would perish and yet survive.

130

Epilogue

May the Meditation of My Mind

There is plenty in the world of psychic phenomena which is naive, neurotic or fraudulent. There is also much that is strange, inexplicable, even wondrous, among the visions, dreams and communications which qualify for the description "paranormal" or — if you use a more question-begging word — "supernatural". In many ways I prefer the word "paranormal" because it contains the possibility that our normality may yet extend to include those psychic phenomena which cannot be explained by today's scientific methods. "Supernatural" implies an interruption of Nature or something that is caused by a power that lies elsewhere than in the world as we know it. That assumption is not always warranted by the evidence, so we should be careful. The theologians who used the idea of a Supreme Being to cover the gaps in human knowledge became aware that it was needed to stretch like an elastic bandage to cover the blanks in human knowledge. Eventually it snapped and discredited the whole idea of a "God of the gaps".

However, it would be a smug person and an ignorant one who assumed that science and technology will go on pushing back frontiers until all that is dark shall be revealed. That naive optimism grew out of a period in which the atom had been split and the brain dissected, when it was believed that both could be broken down into their component parts. However, the matter of which the atom was made proved to be less substantial than was thought and the brain did not quite turn out like a computer — it had a mind of its own. . . .!

I have deliberately played about with puns and ambiguities on the words MIND and MATTER in framing the chapter titles in this book. In some ways they express the ambiguity of the phenomena themselves. There used to be a division of psychic phenomena into MENTAL and PHYSICAL but it is a distinction which is now impossible to maintain because of the inter-relatedness of mind and matter, a facet of so many psi-phenomena. In a materialist universe there is only matter — thoughts and ideas are reduced to the status of neurological patterns in the cerebellum, induced by sensory experience. The materialist view has its counterpart in theology as a god of transcendent reality — a God who is outside matter. This has proved to be a mistake. In describing God as separate from his Creation, theologians have fallen into the trap of their precursors. The consequence of seeing God/spirit or mind/spirit as distinct from matter is to create a two-decker universe, spiritual and material, which effectively withdraws from the no-man's land of inexplicable events. "The Devil divides the world between atheism and superstition," the proverb said. One of the results of nineteenth-century materialism was to drive a wedge between the ways of theology and science — a radical disjunction between faith and reason; sacred and secular; mind and matter. It was a false distinction.

The battlefield of Religion versus Science became a walkover for scientists in the twentieth century. It took a long time for both physicists and theologians to realise, after the discovery of Relativity and the Quantum Theory and now Fundamental Particle Physics, that the enemy have insulted a self-imposed armistice.

Not so on another front. Psychology was trying to establish itself as a science. Like any new convert it was over-zealous and aggressive and kept on fighting long after the sounds of battle had ceased among the physicists, believing that the sun revolved round an earthly trinity of Freud, Watson and Skinner. Followers of Freud explained human behaviour as the result of childhood and sexual conditioning, and the Behaviourist schools of Watson and Skinner worked this into a system with refinements such as genetic influences and chance playing a part — a grim fairy-tale of Mendel and Monod.

Pleasure and reward were apparently the only factors which determined the conduct of twentieth-century Man. The sad plight of this creature, shut in the four dimensions of his

Skinner box-world, was all the more sad because it was the so-called "free-thinkers" of the last century who constructed this model prison. The tools they used were those of scientific method but these admirable methods degenerated into a demarcation-ruled world in which the Physiologist, the Biochemist, the Bio-Physicist, the Psychologist all developed their own Action-Man and dressed him in the vocabulary of their individual discipline.

Sir Cyril Burt said that Psychology, "having first bargained away its soul and then gone out of its mind, seems now, as it faces an untimely end, to have lost all consciousness". He was referring to the tendency to explain behaviour in terms of genetic conditioning or environment, and to regard the brain as a kind of computer. But this mechanistic approach has taken Humpty Dumpty, Homo sapiens, off his perch and dismantled him, only to find that all the pieces cannot be put together again. The whole of man's personality is a lot more than the sum of the parts.

Reductionism is the explanation of a whole in terms of its parts. But explaining each part of the whole man according to different disciplines such as chemistry, physics or biochemistry, is not sufficient to meet the facts. Perhaps the epitaph of these new pharisees concerned with law not Gospel, those sophists who prefer knowledge to truth, was provided by T. H. Huxley, one of the patriarchs of modern science: "It is the customary fate of new truths to begin as heresies and end as superstitions."

Now that the tide is turning against mechanistic, reductionist and behaviourist views of human personality, it is (paradoxically) the new truths of Huxley's era which are being modified, though some scientists cling to them superstitiously and stubbornly. But there also appears to be a new kind of reductionism at work here in parapsychology. It is breaking ethereal Humpty Dumpty into pieces which won't fit together again.

Regrettably, the fight which parapsychology had to establish itself in the freemasonry of science has exacted a price. Experimental approach had to be strictly "scientific" if it was to be accepted as a science. Thus some papers in parapsychology look as if they have been printed by mistake and should have been in a statistical symposium. Of course the tools of modern research must be used and sometimes the vocabulary is specialised, but often the result satisfies very few. In March 1978 an earnest young American, who facially resembled a rodent, tried to persuade the Second International SPR Conference that experiments he had done by threatening a couple of dozen rats with instant death showed a statistical bias towards precognition in those who anticipated their fate. The implicit assumption was that because the probability had been worked out, it carried validity.

The work of Rhine and Soal did much to establish the credibility of psi and this necessarily involved a lot of laborious statistical work. But many experimenters have become obsessed with this — the parameters of their work are too narrow. The big names in the psychical research of yesteryear, men like Lodge and Barrett, kept open minds to possible explanations — they were the renaissance men of this modern science. That remains true of today's leading parapsychologists, men like Bender, Beloff, Price and Hardy, but there are alarming signs that, for parapsychology to establish itself as an academic science, it must follow the reductionist path, sub-dividing into special disciplines and vocabulary. By closing off some avenues of study which are not respectable or by confining research projects to experiments using statistical method, parapsychologists spend their time straining at gnats (or should it be rats?) and swallowing camels. Or if they exclude too many variables because they are not amenable to laboratory study they narrow the possible results so much that the camel will never get through the needle. However, I believe that para-psychology offers the unique possibility of being the catalyst of a new synthesis in science. It could be a means for the clinical psychiatrist and the physicist, as well as other branches of science, to put Humpty Dumpty together again.

Breakthrough

The range of psi phenomena covered by this book is incomplete. Nor do the categories and divisions of subjects fall easily into place. The EVP could have been placed so easily in the chapter on Survival. The poltergeist is perhaps a particular instance of PK. Apparitions could be a mixture of PK and clairvoyance, with post- and pre-cognition entering the picture. Reincarnation could be intermittent survival or clairvoyance. Only metal-bending is *pure* PK.

But this does not take us very far. Merely giving names to phenomena does not explain them. The overlaps between apparitions and poltergeists and between EVPs and OOBEs and survival incidents, does not give us a full picture of what is happening or any clearer account of how these basic principles work.

Perhaps an analogy might help. Imagine the brain as a radio/ cassette recorder. It can receive ordinary sense impressions on the "Medium Wave" through eyes, ears, nose, mouth and touch. It can record these and have recall playback. These are available to be played back on other sets but when sufficiently excited by a programme it succeeds in transmitting it on a "Short Wave" band to those who have the ability to tune in. On other occasions it can receive "Long Wave" transmissions of events which are going on and not capable of being received on the "Medium Wave". But somewhere in the BBC, producers are compiling future programmes and test transmissions are being done on the "VHF" waveband and occasionally if a radio is tuned to VHF it will pick up fragments of programmes which will later be available in a coherent and full form on medium wave. This analogy is not meant to suggest that our picture of the world is pre-ordained by people in the BBC — much as some discontented souls would like to think — but to point out that this radio "mind", which is a piece of relatively commonly available apparatus, provides a model of consciousness simultaneous on different levels; recalls of the past; trans- missions of memories and their accessibility to others; and fragmentary knowledge of impending events.

I further suggest that three questions are basic to discussing these four facets of psi: what is mind? what is matter? what is time?

By reducing the parameters to mind, matter and time, we cannot reduce the difficulties. We see that because of the inherent difficulties of understanding the nature of these basic concepts of parapsychology, we are not likely to reach a complete solution.

Substance of the Matter
Even if we were to seek a materialist solution in terms of the

physical forces we know and can measure. Even if we could find that the brain was another version of our radio model with computing facilities built in. Even if the brain could be reduced to a known content of memories and conditioning reflexes, with certain electromagnetic waves and charges running through a complex of chemical substances, whose molecular behaviour was predictable — even if (and a big IF it is) this was so, *logical determinancy* is still lacking — the ability to predict exactly how the person would behave or think. The very fact that the brain is being observed alters the objectivity of the data. The experimenter is part of the experiment. This kind of neo-Cartesian principle — "I think, therefore, I influence what I am thinking about", can also be stated in the sixteenth-century proverb, "The eye that sees all things sees not itself".

This principle applies not only in psychology but also in physics, where the observer can only describe events RELATIVE to himself and not in ABSOLUTE terms, as in Einstein's Principle of Relativity. On the atomic level the Uncertainty Principle of Heisenberg declares that any attempt to describe the speed and exact position of a sub-atomic particle is futile. Either we know its position or its speed, but not both at once. This inherent fuzziness is at the heart of any attempt to get outside the 4-D universe of space and time.

Unless our "doors of perception" are cleansed we will have great difficulty in appreciating which is the REAL world. The phrase belongs to William Blake, the mystic poet. Who is to say the world he sees is not as real or true as the one we live in?

The Omega Factor

In "Paracelsus", Browning wrote of Truth as within ourselves, hemmed in by the gross flesh, and Knowing, rather than effecting entry for a light supposed to be without, "consists in opening out a way whence the imprisoned splendour may escape". If we approach the quotation from a materialist or a gnostic angle we will see survival of death as a bird fleeing a cage, a prisoner escaping a cell, or a soul rising from a tomb. But suppose instead that in dying we are completing the pattern of nature which begins as *alpha* and ends as *omega* — the Greek letter Ω which is also a symbol of a wave. The wave form is indeed a symbol of our form of life. It is the parabola which arches up like a high-jumper in youth

136

until he touches the peak, when powers begin to fail, and he falls down again.

Jung observes that the mental life of an individual is also a parabola, and good mental health in the latter half is dependent on the way we accept and face up to the inevitability of death. The wave is a paradigm of many facets of nature which are cyclic. The movement of the stars and earth itself; the transmission of heat and light and sound are all cycles or wave forms. So is even matter itself — the mathematical symbol for matter in its smallest sub-atomic form is something known as the "Schrodinger Wave Equation" and was derived from Einstein's Theories of Relativity. Einstein's great work was to show that we live in a great ocean of gravity and electromagnetism — a *field*, through which these forces travel in the form of waves. It was believed that electromagnetic waves travelled through an invisible substance called "ether", which permeated the universe and permitted the passage of such waves in the way that water transmits waves across the ocean. Half-baked theories such as the spiritualist writings of J. Arthur Findlay cling to this concept of "ether" as the medium or curtain between "this world" and the "spirit world". With the famous Michelson-Morley experiment, ether was rendered not only invisible but impossible. A new and more exciting prospect was opened up — that the energy which the wave carried and the energy which caused it to begin in motion were all one and the same thing, expressed in the simple formula which was to prove explosive in its implications:

$E = Mc^2$ (E—Energy, M—Mass, c—the speed of light).

Sub-atomic particles, the building-blocks of matter, have thus been reduced to wave equations. These shadowy realities expressed by equations can only be seen by a spy-in-the-corner device which traces their path through bubbles of condensation in a cloud chamber. Some particles have yet to be seen by even this delicate method — they are theoretical and the scientist has to believe that they exist in the way that the theologian needs the idea of a soul. The theoretical particles help to explain certain aspects of the behaviour of the nucleus. Now and then techniques advance a little — (better technology makes better electron microscopes, faster particle accelerators, more efficient cloud chambers) — and the

137

hypothetical particle is "discovered" — only to be broken down within a year or so into other types of particles. Similarly, the philosophies and metaphysics systems come and go in fashion, attributing Platonic, Aristotelian or Cartesian qualities to the soul, according to what fits with the current symbols of that epoch.

Modern physics has evolved a new vocabulary. "Quarks" are thought to be the smallest of the sub-atomic particles which themselves are given "strangeness numbers" and possess a property called "charm". Theology has its symbols of spirit and soul, and its doctrines of grace and atonement. We should be no more harsh on the theologians who cannot describe the final absolute laws of Divine Purpose than we would be on scientists who cannot give the final answers. Both sets of scholars are limited by their apparatus (technology and the human body respectively) and by the inadequacy of their symbols.

New Symbols for Old

The Theory of Relativity has had profound implications on our view of the universe. It has demonstrated that the basic qualities and quantities which describe matter are inter-changeable and relate to each other in simple but profound equations. In one view the universe is like a clock emitting pulses of light and running down. In another view it will stand still if the clock is stopped by exceeding the speed of light. What then of the past, present and future? It is tempting to speculate about parallel universes of reality in which Charles I's head is being chopped off and the pyramids are still being built. They cannot be proved. But there is enough theory of modern science to make Horatio think twice about his philosophy — and enough in the survival literature to make Hamlet think again about life as inexorable descent into nihilistic oblivion.

The results of parapsychology research may seem to have absorbed religion and demythologised "mind" to a wavy line on a graph of brain activity. But the time-honoured myths of the Bible are not brushed aside as easily as that and keep resurfacing, albeit in new forms. A profound revolution is going on in our pseudo-literate world, unfamiliar with the old myths of the Bible, which is re-mythologising new ones. The oldest parts of the Old Testament are stories and legends told round the camp-fires of the ancient caravan trails. The story of Tiamat, the Babylonian monster of the deep, was rewritten as Noah's Flood and later as Jonah's whale. Modern Man was now re-mythologised Tiamat as "Jaws". Sodom and Gomorrah has become "The Towering Inferno".

I have heard the blessing which Jacob stole from Esau identified by a Hebrew professor at Glasgow University with psi-ability. This BERACHAH (Vital Force) may be what is now called an "energy body". It would provide an ancient equivalent of the "Star Wars" greeting, "May the force be with you". The modern demi-gods whose chariots are UFOs and have "Close Encounters" of a commercial kind with Mr Von Daniken and Mr Geller, can be an enjoyable fiction if we are prepared to give them as much historical credence as we would the visions of St John the Divine on Patmos. It is when myth is confused with history that our credulity cannot cope. Yet myth is historical in the sense of inspiring and being inspired by men throughout history, and the powerful myths and symbols of religion and magic have a great deal to do with the world of the psyche.

A Clash of Symbols

Parapsychology has arrived on the doorstep of the 'eighties, and it has developed significantly. After languishing as a pseudo-scientist for so long, armed with his EEG and RNG machines, the parapsychologist now occupies what Wolfgang Pauli called "the border territory between physics and psychology".

An American philosopher has described psychoanalysis as a collection of theories without any facts, and para-psychology as a collection of facts without any theory. At least he concedes that the facts are facts and not self-delusions or fraud. But since it is doubtful, if you have read this far, that you take that view, I will make the assumption that whatever you think of the evidence cited for psychic phenomena, you will concede that it is fact not fiction.

I am not suggesting that the phenomena described in this book, or even the salutary advances in parapsychological research and in public interest in it, constitute a new body of knowledge. But we have reached the point when the evidence for "psi" has been established beyond all reasonable doubt. Yet the whole subject still languishes as a pseudo-science and a refuge for cranks. Reactions to the paranormal can still be divided into X, Y and Z — disbelievers, questioners and believers.

Z is for Zany

These are the eccentric or impressionable people who "need" to believe in something, and the something often turns out to be the nearest peg on which they can hang their big black pointed hats. These people still hanker after the awesome delights of the comic books which they read as children and which were peopled by green men from Mars or aliens with superhuman powers. Finally, this category includes the mentally weak and the neurotic whose subconscious sculpts their fears and repressions into hideous forms, some genuinely paranormal and some simply high-flown imagination. The Z person is the popular caricature of the psychic but it is becoming less relevant.

X stands for No

The X person is the disbeliever who refuses to accept any sort of paranormal phenomena as either possible or having happened. He belongs to the small (three per cent in a *New Scientist* poll) but hard core of sceptics who act as necessary watchdogs, lest any psychic researcher swallow too many red herrings, but who sometimes end up by labelling all experimenters and subjects as cheats and frauds in a frantic attempt to say nothing psychic has happened. The have exposed many frauds and, like James Randi, the American illusionist and magician, have often been able to replicate the phenomena of famous psychics by means of trickery. But if one swallow does not make a summer, one cheat does not render all the evidence useless. Nor does the fact that it is possible to replicate certain happenings by trickery necessarily imply they cannot happen by paranormal means.

We all start with certain assumptions about the nature of the world. These are likely to colour our observations and conclusions drawn from them. If one experimenter believes in psi and another does not, they are both likely to get different results from the same experiment. (It has been shown that some experimenters act as dampers, others as catalysts to good results.) The Philip group who "manufactured" their own ghost, regarded belief in the possibility of achieving their task as essential. This is frustrating for the scientist who believes (vainly if the best philosophers of science are correct) in the existence of absolute objective truth about the physical world. This attitude determines what kind of results he will get. The X person is sometimes driven, by phenomena which can't be conjured, to postulate hallucination and self-deception or explanations which demand so many coincidences that they become more difficult to believe than the original psychic event. Even if a Uri Geller, or a Mathew Manning, or an Ingo Swann has a great deal to gain financially and in publicity from his psychic gifts, it should be said that the best (and biggest) source of evidence is from reluctant witnesses whose experience was often involuntary. (Who would wish for a poltergeist to take up residence in his or her home?) If, like James Randi, you start from the position "you may be sure that (it) is done by trickery", without having seen the event in question, it is doubtful whether you have quality of open mind necessary to undertake any scientific evaluation.

Y and Wherefore
Where the already trodden path of scientific laws diverges from the evidence for psychic phenomena, the challenge is to explain the latter in terms of the former. The integration of the two into a single theory has so far eluded parapsychologists. There are those who, despite being convinced atheists, are prepared to admit that something in the physical substrate of the mind is able to generate psi-phenomena, a kind of human radar, a sixth sense like that which guides a bee to its hive or a bat to its cave.

There are others who have concluded that psi-phenomena have demonstrated, albeit in a scrambled form, survival of bodily death. But it is the same evidence which is used to support the idea of a surviving spirit and a sixth sense. It is possible that both are true, but at the moment the evidence is not so clear as to settle the question beyond argument.

Behaviourist psychologists say that those who disagree with them have been conditioned to feel that way. In philosophy, the linguistic analysts can only answer questions which have meaning within their systems of values, so they cannot tell if there is something called "true love". If a mathematician seeks a solution to an equation which requires numbers like —1, but refuses to admit that such imaginary numbers exist, then he cannot give an answer within his frame of reference. The same difficulty is found in parapsychology which uses elements of psychology, philosophy and science. The result is that the sceptics have ended up with trivial data (graphs and probabilities) and the believers have ended up finding gods who have been made in their own mirror image. In dealing with psychic phenomena, the question "WHY?" is less innocent than it seems. Who asks it, and how he reacts to the answer may well have a part to play in the answer he gets.

In the 1920s Gurdjieff threw out the challenge to his followers, "Do you wish to die like a man or perish like a dog?". The fact that man can ask the question and be able to influence the outcome may well be an answer in itself. It may also suggest that the mind has a much greater potential than we give it a chance to display. None of us likes the thought that the human psyche (which gave psi its name) may be like an extra faculty in rats which enables them to find their way out of the maze. I hope that when you have traced your way through the maze of evidence for psychical phenomena in this book, you will agree that although the mind/body/spirit trinity may not be fully understood, its complexity and mystery must inspire awe. For some, that awe will be a *preparatio evangelica*, the seeds of which will bear fruit in religious faith. For others, it will make them think that there is more in heaven and earth than is dreamt of in their philosophy. To those who still think that psychic phenomena are of no earthly use and dispute that they even exist, I would direct a remark by Lord McLeod of Fuinary. He had been describing a life-changing event of near-miraculous proportions. "If you think that's a coincidence," he explained, "I hope you have a very dull life."

Glossary

ESP	Extra-sensory perception. Experience of an object, state, event or influence without sensory contact.
Clairvoyance	Extra-sensory perception of objects or objective events.
Telepathy	Extra-sensory perception of the mental state or activity of another person.
PK	Psychokinesis. Direct mental but non-muscular influence exerted by a subject on an external physical process, condition, object.
psi	General term for ESP and extra-sensorimotor activity. Includes PK, telepathy, clairvoyance, precognition and postcognition (the paranormal knowledge of past or future events beyond the range of inference or memory).
Parapsychology	The science which deals with psi.
Paranormal	Faculties and phenomena which are beyond present understanding of cause and effect.
Supernatural	See Paranormal. The former is sometimes preferred because it does not contain the implication that there is an order of events which are "above" natural laws.
OOBE	Out-of-Body Experience. The purported detachment, voluntary or involuntary, of part of the conscious mind from the physical body while remaining connected to it throughout the experience.
Medium	A person who perceives and demonstrates paranormal faculties regularly or at will. Also known as "psychics" or "sensitives".
SC	State of Consciousness. ASC = Altered SC. dSC = discrete or detached SC.
TC	Transpersonal Consciousness. SC which includes awareness beyond the individual and personal; and occasionally provides knowledge which could not be gained through the senses.